CAMBRIDGE LIBRARY COLLECTION

Books of enduring scholarly value

European History

This series includes accounts of historical events and movements by eye-witnesses and contemporaries, as well as landmark studies that assembled significant source materials or developed new historiographical methods. It covers the social and political history of continental Europe from the Renaissance to the end of the nineteenth century, and its broad range includes works on Russia and the Balkans, revolutionary France, the papacy and the inquisition, and the Venetian state archives.

The Jewish Question, 1875–1884

Although born in Australia, the historian and folklorist Joseph Jacobs (1854–1916) spent his adult years in England and America. Educated at Cambridge and Berlin, he came to public attention in 1882 following the publication in *The Times* of a series of articles on the persecution of Jews in Russia that had followed the assassination of Alexander II. The Mansion House Committee to aid the Jews of Russia was established as a result of these articles. In 1885 he published this book, listing all the printed works on the 'Jewish Question' that had appeared in the previous decade. It is notable that those items originating in Germany form the bulk of the bibliography, providing as much material as all other countries combined. Revealing in its scope, this has been described as the most important contemporary bibliography on the subject.

The Jewish Question
1875–1884

Bibliographical Hand-List

COMPILED BY JOSEPH JACOBS

CAMBRIDGE UNIVERSITY PRESS

Cambridge, New York, Melbourne, Madrid, Cape Town,
Singapore, São Paolo, Delhi, Mexico City

Published in the United States of America by Cambridge University Press, New York

www.cambridge.org
Information on this title: www.cambridge.org/9781108053655

© in this compilation Cambridge University Press 2013

This edition first published 1885
This digitally printed version 2013

ISBN 978-1-108-05365-5 Paperback

THE

JEWISH QUESTION

1875—1884.

BIBLIOGRAPHICAL HAND-LIST.

COMPILED BY
JOSEPH JACOBS, B.A.,
LATE SCHOLAR OF ST. JOHN'S COLLEGE, CAMBRIDGE.

*Les ennemis du judaïsme, regardez-y de près, vous verrez
que ce sont en général des ennemis de l'esprit moderne.*
RENAN.

LONDON:
TRÜBNER AND CO., LUDGATE HILL.
1885.
All Rights Reserved.

HERTFORD:

PRINTED BY STEPHEN AUSTIN AND SONS.

FRATRIBUS

SYDNEY EDWIN LOUIS

PATERNO MUNERE

FUNCTIS

HAS PRIMITIAS.

Then went the Jury out whose names were, Mr. *Blind-man*, Mr. *No-good*, Mr. *Malice*, Mr. *Love-lust*, Mr. *Live-loose*, Mr. *Heady*, Mr. *Highmind*, Mr. *Enmity*, Mr. *Lyar*, Mr. *Cruelty*, Mr. *Hate-light* and Mr. *Implacable*; who every one gave his private Verdict against him amongst themselves, and afterwards unanimously concluded to bring him in guilty before the Judge. And first among themselves, Mr. *Blind-man*, the Foreman, said, *I see clearly that this man is an Heretick.* Then said Mr. *No-good, Away with such a fellow from the earth. Ay,* said Mr. *Malice, for I hate the very looks of him.* Then said Mr. *Love-lust, I could never endure him. Nor I,* said Mr. *Live-loose, for he would always be condemning my way. Hang him,* said Mr. *Heady. A sorry scrub,* said Mr. *High-mind. My heart riseth against him,* said Mr. *Enmity. He is a Rogue,* said Mr. *Lyar. Hanging is too good for him,* said Mr. *Cruelty. Let us dispatch him out of the way,* said Mr. *Hate-light.* Then said Mr. *Implacable, Might I have all the world given me, I could not be reconciled to him; therefore let us forthwith bring him in guilty of death.*

BUNYAN *Pilgrim's Progress.*

PREFACE.

In the following list an attempt has been made to collect together all the literary productions emanating from either side in the so-called Jewish Question under its Protean aspects in Europe and America during the decade 1875-1884. It is intended to include books, pamphlets, speeches, reports of meetings and societies, anti-Semitic newspapers and articles in non-Jewish periodicals, especially when signed. Articles in Jewish papers (of which a list is given in Singer 480) are excluded, except when reprinted, and the Broadsheets (108-120), Posters (389-401), and pieces of Music (318-9), are only selected specimens. As a clue to general press utterances the index to the *Times* (332) may suffice.

The arrangement is alphabetical under authors' names, the anonymous articles being collected together, also in alphabetical order, under that heading (11-76, 532-8). The following Analysis may serve as a rough guide to the multifarious contents of the list, the anonyma being indicated by short titles in italics, the remainder by author's name. Numbers are added where doubt might occur. Asterisks mark specially important or interesting works.

A. General.

A. *Andree, Henne-am-Rhyn, *Israel und Gojim.* **P.**
Astruc (538), *Darmstatter, Ellenberger, Levi (562),
Reports—Jew. Soc. (409–12), Scherdlin, Schleinitz. **C.**
Kellog, Frank (549).

B. Germany.

I. General (foreign). **A.** 'Germ. Home Life' (368), G.
Richard. **P.** Boole, Bourdeau, Coen, *Correspondant*
(55), Daniow, Eisler, Fastigato, Franck, Gonne, Grant,
Hall (554), Rahlenbach, Salzburger, Sulzberger, Taussig,
*Schuster, *Valbert, Wolf.

II. History. A. *Bankberger, Calendar, Lehnhardt.
[In the Past] Dreydroff, Jungfer, Wyking. **P.** *Bresslau.
[In Past] Berliner, Dessauer.
Republications. **A.** Hauff, Simplicissimus. **P.** Manasseh
ben Israel, Macaulay.
Attitude of eminent persons. (Luther) **A.** *Luther* ; (Less-
ing), **A.** *Dühring. **P.** *Hinrichtung* ; (Lassalle). **P.**
Ferdinand ; (Auerbach), **P.** Stein. (Bismarck), **P.** *Bis-
marck's ;* (Bluntschli), **P.** *Offenes ;* (Du Bois). **P.** *Ein
Wort ;* (Liszt), Sagittarius ; (Schleiden). **P.** *Professor
Schleiden ;* (Wagner). **A.** Wagner. **P.** Cassel ; (Zöllner).
P. *Herr Prof. Zöllner.* See *Agitation* IV. (3) and
Defence V. (1) and (2).

III. Press. For general press see Index to *Times* (332)
1880–81 *sub. voc.* ' Germany.' Also note before 335,
*Broadsheets 111–2, Newspapers 335–42, and Periodicals
374a–380, esp. **Deutsche Wacht, Kultur Kämpfer,
Wahrheit, and Schmeitzner (569). **P.** List of Jewish
papers at end of *Singer (480). **C.** Conversionist
papers in Roi 438a p. 7.

IV. The Agitation. A. Anon. *Fremdlinge, Manifest, Mauscheljude,* *Neupalestina, Semita, Sittenlehre, Studien,* Brake, Broadsheets 108, 117, 118, Osman Bey, Cunow, *Dühring, Ernst, Frey, *Förster, Gauvain, Gronsilliers, *Henrici, Heyse, P. Köhler, Naudh, Paulakowsky, Perrot, Reports—Meetings 413, 414, 416, Reymond, Rohan, Rüppel, Schrenzel, Simplicissimus, *Statutes (489), *Trapp, Wahrmund, *Waldegg, Wasinski, Wedell, *Willmanns. Esp. (1) *MARR. **A.** Perinhardt, Reymond. **P.** *Wucher,* Siegfried, Stein. (2) *STÖCKER. **A.** Broad-sht. 110, Diehl, Posters 390–1. **P.** *Briefwechsel, Offener, Theorien,* Baumgarten, Bernstein, Cohn, Donner, Kaufmann, Klein, Kleist, Leschmann, Letson, Müller, *Times* (332, 1883), Oppenheimer, Parl. Rep. (364), Ronge (568a), Rudoll. (3) *TREITSCHKE. **A.** Endner, Naudh. **P.** Börne, *Bresslau, *Cassel, *Cohen, Glück, Graetz, *Lazarus, S. Meyer, *Mommsen, Nadyr, Neubauer, Neumann, Oppenheimer, Philadelphus.

V. The Defence. [*Jews.*] **P.** Anon. *Schuldig,* *Bamberger, *Bresslau, Donner, Friedeburg, Goldsmidt, Freund, Grünbaum, Jolenburg, Judäus, Lehman, Lewin, Maier, Mandl, Mainz, Münz, Neustadt, Neumann (566), Reichenbach, Rosenberg, Siegfried, *Steinthal, Sulzbach, Willheimer. Esp. (1) *LAZARUS. **A.** Brdsht. 108-2. **P.** Cohen. See also above IV. 1–3. [*Self-criticism.*] **P.** Cohen, Friedeberg, Moses, Rubens, Schreiber. [*Gentiles.*] **P.** Anon. *Apologie, Die Juden, Ob der Jude,* *Beck, *Döllinger, Ave-Lallemont, Gruber, *Hillebrand, Hommel, Kelchner, Kalthoff, Kolkmann, Lichtenstein, Norton, Piton, *Protest, Revel, *Schleiden, Scholl, Stöpel, Esp. (2) *MOMMSEN. **P.** Protest. **A.** Amitti, *Th. Mommsen,* Treitschke. (3) *CASSEL. **A.** Berthold.

VI. Political. A. (Conserv.) Anon. *ABC, Votum,* Broadsheets 109, 110, 113, 114, 118, 120, Frantz, *Glagau,

R. Meyer, Newspapers, Parl. Reports, 360-3, Posters, 390-4, 399, Reports—Meetings, 413-4. P. (Nat. Lib.), Anon. *Bismarck's*, Broadsheets 119, Posters, Reports 415, 417, Richter.

VII. Economic. A. Anon. **Aera*, Bankberger, Germanicus, Heffel, Maurer, Porsch, Waldegg. **P.** Anon. *Geldmacht*, *Rost. See *Agitation* IV. [*Bourse*.] **A.** *Aera*, Bankberger, Chevalier, Germanicus. [*Usury*.] **A.** *Studien*. **P.** *Wucher*, Bodek, Löwy, Wolff.

VIII. Social. A. *Fremdlinge, Social-politische*, Gutmuths, Hammer, *Hartmann, *Hellenbach. **P.** *Vom Judenthum*, Freund, Kolkmann, Marbach, Witt. [*Criminal*]. **A.** *Ahnensaal*, **Antheil*. **P.** Ave-Lallemant, *Löwenfeldt [*Mixed marriages*]. **A.** Maas, Rohan. **P.** Müller, Rauchmann [*Immigration from Russia*], **A.** Treitschke. **P.** *Neumann.

IX. Religious. A. Broadsheet 115, 117, Hartmann, Heman, *Heuch, Ludolf, Rocholl. **P.** *Briefwechsel*. [*Conversion*.] **C.** Anon. *Judenfrage, Reine Mosaismus, Wahre Lösung, Ein Wort*, Christleib, *Delitzsch, Gerhard, Janasz, *Le Roi, Plath, Schüler, Somerville. **P.** *Warum treten*, *Grünebaum, Molchow, *Singer. [*Sermons*.] **P.** Fränkl, Hildesheimer Kaufmann, Landsberger, Ritter. [*Talmud*.] **A.** *Aberglaubische, Sittenlehre, Talmud*, Daab, Ecker (546), Gildemeister (551), *Justus. **P.** Duschak, Fischer, Hirsch (556), *Hoffmann (557), Jellinek, Joel (558), *Lewin (563). [*Blood Accusation*.] **A.** *Gebrauchen*, see Austria.

X. Professional. [*University*] **A.** *Antisemitische, Luther, Studentische*, Fischer, M., Reports, Siecke, **P.** Spangenburg. [*Legal*] **A.** *Jüd. Referendarius*, Grumbkow. **P.** *Jüd. Referendarius*, Zander. [*Medical*] **A.** Richard. [*Press*] **A.** Junius Lerique, Wuttke. **P.** *Vom Judenthum*. [*Music*] **A.** *Juden*, Sagittarius, Wagner.

XI. Literary Treatment. [*Novels.*] **P.** *Apion* (532), *Laube (560). **C.** Meuthner. [*Drama.*] **A.** Diehl. [*Essay.*] **P.** Amyntor, Grätz. [*Comic Poetry.*] **A.** *Hep-hep*, *Zeitgedichte.* Calendar, Frey, *Kuhn, Lindauer, Simplex, Songbook. **P.** Vindex *Sanders, Capilleri, Erichson.

XII. Miscellaneous. [*Trials.*] **A.** Grumkow. **P.** *Jüd. Referendarius*, Parl. Reports, Rodkinsohn, Sello (570). [**Curiosities.*] **A.** Advts., Backhaus, Beta, Calendar, Cards, Directory, Gronsilliers, Illustrations, Medals, Music, Post-cards, Railway, Song-book. See *Poetry* XI. [*Unknown and Miscellaneous.*] Anders, *Hetz*, Brake, Enodatus, Grau, Heyse, Lippert.

C. Austria-Hungary.

I. General. A. Austriacus, Farkas, Istoczy, Lázár, Matok, Newspapers — Austria, Observator, Platter, Schnörerer, Simonyi, Stanojevic, Statutes, Wieneger ; **P.** Baum (540), Bloch, Kohn, Jellinek, Singer, *Wertheimer. *Istoczy* (534), *Magyar* (535), *Zsidokerdes* (538).

II. Blood Accusation. P. *Blood-accusation, Blutbeschuldigung, *Christliche, Teufelskralle*, Delitzsch, Duschak, Friedlander (548), Groebler (552), *Guidetti (553), Güdemann, Hamburger, Oort, Renan, Rodkinsohn, Spitzer, *Wright. **A.** *Gebrauchen*, Neofito, esp. *Rohling. **P.** Bloch, Ellenberger, *Delitzsch, Fraenkel, Lippe (564). Löwy, Kayserling, Nobel.

III. Tisza-Eszlar Trial. A. *Esther*, Morel, Donath (novel), M., Marczianyi, Onody, **P.** *Eingabe* (533), *Mord, *Process*, Geist (550), Gladius, Herzfeld, Morell, Reuss, Schönwald, *Valbert, *Times* 332, 1883.

D. Russia.

I. General. A. *Brafmann, Basily, Brüggen, *Ragozin. Reports. **P.** Autoemancipation, Barine, Eismann (547),

Goldenburg, Jurisconsultus, *Lazarus, Lipschutz, Rülf, Schwabacher, Sokolow, *San Donato, Serberling. [*Blood Accusation.*] **A.** Ljutostanski. **P.** *Chwolson.

II. Persecutions. P. *Judenhetze, Persecution,* *Persecution* (52), *Russian Atrocities, Russischen,* Cox, E. Lazarus, Official Papers, 347-50, 352, Parl. Reports, Swinburne, Szinnesy. [*Relief.*] Comtes-Rendus, Goldman, Reports, Hugo, Rülf. [*The Exodus.*] Comtes Rendus, Friedländer, Moreniss. [**Curiosities.*] Altlass, Campbell, Dictionary, Friemann, Poster.

E. Roumania.

A. Brouner, * Cressulesco, Rizu-Lambru, Rosetti. **P.** Adrian, *Conventions, Question, Petition.* Bassin, *Bluntschli, Canini, Kauffman, *Loeb. Offic. Papers 346, 351a. Parl. Rep., Reports. Schein (Blood-accusation).

F. France.

A. *Question juive,* Newspapers—France, Renan, Weiss. **P.** Cleef, Hugo, Mazaroz, Newspapers, Renan, *Saint-Yves, Scherdlin.

G. England.

A. See *Times,* 332, 1876-7, Hyndman, Laister, Period. *Fortnightly,* *Spectator.* Esp. *Smith, answered by **P.** *Adler, Eliot, Montefiore (cf. Cobbe), Schwab, Wolf. **P.** Fremantle, Oliphant, Salaman, Samuel. [*Curiosities.*] **A.** MacDonald, Newspapers, 331.

H. Other Countries.

[*Denmark*] Wolff. [*Morocco*] Offic. Papers (351b). [*United States*] Morais.

In all the list contains 1230 items in the following languages arranged in order of frequency : German, English,

French, Hebrew, Hungarian, Roumanian, Italian, Russian, Dutch, Spanish, Polish, Danish. Of these, however, 417 are press notices tabulated under Nos. 52, 332, 335, 371b, 371c, 379a. Of the remainder 496 are pamphlets (34 being translations), of which 186 are Antisemitic, 295 Prosemitic, and 15 Conversionist. I cannot refrain from pointing out the obvious moral of these figures, that the over-eagerness of Jews to defend themselves has clearly only served to add fuel to the flames by which they were being roasted.

Extensive as it is, the list, drawn up far from the centre of the conflict, is probably not complete : no bibliography ever was. But I trust no important utterance has been omitted, as I have been favoured by Messrs. Dulau and Co. with access to a very extensive collection of German pamphlets in their possession, while Prof. Kaufmann of Buda-Pesth has kindly favoured me with the Hungarian items to which his initial is attached. I have also received much aid from three lists in Steinschneider's *Heb. Bibliog.* vols. xx. and xxi., as well as from the excellent bibliographical lists of M. Isidore Loeb in the *Revue des Etudes juives.* It seemed to me worth while aiming at relative completeness, as the only notice that most of the works mentioned in this list deserve is that of being included in some such bibliography.

JOSEPH JACOBS.

88, SHIRLAND GARDENS, W.,
   Aug. 1885.

THE JEWISH QUESTION,

1875–1883.

Adler, Dr. Hermann, Delegate Chief Rabbi.

1. Can Jews be Patriots? In *Nineteenth Century*, April, 1878, pp. 637-646. **P.**
[Answering Goldwin Smith, No. 481.]

2. Jews and Judaism ; a Rejoinder. In *Nineteenth Century*, July, 1878, pp. 133-150 **P.**
[Replying to Goldwin Smith, No. 482.]

3. Recent Phases of Judæophobia. In *Nineteenth Century*, December, 1881, pp. 813-829. **P.**
[In answer to Goldwin Smith, No. 483, and calling attention to Russian outbreaks. Answered by same, No. 484.]

Adrian, General G.

4. Quelques mots sur la question Israélite en Roumanie. Paris, 1879 (Parent). 8vo. pp. 16. **P.**

Advertisements.

5. Gustav Kölzsch, Juwelier, Berlin. . . . . Specialität : Antisemitische Berloques. **A.**
[At end of *"Kehraus,"* No. 124.]

6. Ferner sind durch die Expedition der Wahrheit, Berlin, C., Schlossplatz, 4, zu beziehen : Antisemitische Berloque-Medaillen 1, 2, 3. Levy, Cohen, Meyer . . . in Silber emaillirt : Lilly-Händschen. Züchtigungsmittel für schamlose Verleumder (Lilly Lehmann contra Davidsohn), in reinem Silber. Der so beliebte polnische Jude in höherer Stellung, stark versilbert. 3 Mark. **A.**
[At end of *"Kehraus,"* No. 124; illustrations of lockets given.]

I

Advertisements—*continued.*

Amitti, K. [=Manus Katz, q.v.]

7. Zur Kritik der Antisemiten und—Semiten. Ein Beitrag zur Bekämpfung der von Prof. Mommsen erwähnten "Antipathischen Gefühle " gegen die letzteren. Leipzig, 1881 (Morgenstern). 8vo. pp. 40. **A.**

[*Cf.* Mommsen, No. 311.]

Amyntor, Gerhard von [Pseudonym for v. Gerhard.]

8. Eine moderne Abendgesellschaft. Berlin, 1881 (Issleib). 8vo. pp. 64. **P.**

[Dialogue giving views pro and contra.]

Anders, R. J.

9. Held und seine Wahnsinns-Theorien. Berlin, 1880. 8vo. pp. 16. [H. B. xx. 76.] **A.**

Andree, Richard.

10. Zur Volkskunde der Juden. Mit einer Karte über die Verbreitung der Juden in Mittel-Europa. Bielefeld und Leipzig, 1881 (Velhagen u. Klasing). 8vo. pp. viii. and 296, and Map. **A.**

[Statistics and extracts from travellers.]

Anonymous. [Alphabetically arranged without regard to definite article.]

See *Advertisements—Broadsheets—Cards—Comptes Rendus—Calendar—Dictionary— Directory—Illustrations— Music—Official Papers —Parliamentary Reports — Post Cards—Posters—Protest — Reports—Songbook— Statutes.* See *Pseudonyms.* See *Newspapers—Periodicals.*

11. A B C für Conservative Wähler, herausgegeben unter Mitwirkung namhafter Conservativen. Berlin, 1881. (M. Schulze). 8vo. pp. 56 **A.**

[Political and Social Topics arranged Alphabetically: *e.g.*— Actien Gesellschaften, Antisemitenliga, Christenthum, Gründerschwindel, Schmähsucht der Juden, Zeitungen (warning against "Vossische Zeitung," "Berliner.Tageblatt," etc.,etc.) Seemingly in answer to A B C für Liberale.]

Anonymous—*continued.*

12a. Actenmässige Darstellung der jüdischen Zustände in Russland, 1883. Hannover (Typ. Gesell. der Prov. Hannover). 4to. pp. 14. **P.**
[Statistics favourable to Russian Jews.]

12. Die Abergläubischen Religionsgebraüche der Talmudischen Juden, von ihren Rabbinern vorgeschrieben, aber nur hier und da durchwegs noch beobachtet. Bern, 1880 (?). [H. B. xxi. 87.] **A.**

13. Die Aera Bleichröder-Delbrück-Camphausen. Separat-Abdruck der fünf Aera-Artikel aus der *Kreuz-Zeitung*, nebst Literatur darüber und einem Vor- und Nachwort des Verfassers. Berlin, 1876. (M. A. Niendorf.) 8vo. pp. 77. **A.**

14. Die Antisemiten-Agitation und die deutsche Studentenschaft. Zweite umgearbeitete Auflage. Göttingen, 1881. (Peppmüller). 8vo. pp. 23. **A.**

15. Apologie der Juden von einem Germanen. [H. B. xxi. 47.] **P.**
(In Franz Stöpel's Maître, Bd. I., Heft. 3. Berlin, 1880.)

16. "Autoemancipation." Mahnruf an seine Stammesgenossen von einem russischen Juden. Berlin, 1882 (Issleib). 8vo. pp. 36. **P.**

17. Bismarck's Verhältniss zum Glauben insbesondere zum Judenthum, in vier Kapiteln: Glaube, Aberglaube, Toleranz, Vorurtheile. Leipzig, 1879. 8vo. pp. 16. [H. B. xx. 29.] **P.**
(Abdruck aus "Israelit. Wochenschrift.")

17a. The "Blood Accusation," its Origin and Occurrence during the Middle Ages. An Historical Commentary on the Tisza-Eszlar Trial. London, 1883 (A. I. Myers). 8vo. pp. 12. **P.**
[Reprinted from the *Jewish Chronicle*, June 29, 1883. First two articles by present compiler.]

17b. Die Blutbeschuldigung gegen die Juden von christlicher Seite beurtheilt. Wien, 1882 (Steyrmühl). **P.**
[Similar to "Christliche Zeugnisse," No. 19, with the addition of an opinion from M. Renan and other matter.]

Anonymous—*continued.*

18. Ein Briefwechsel zwischen Jolenberg und Stöcker.
Berlin, 1880. 8vo. pp. 15. [H. B. xxi. 48.]   **P.**

18a. Briefwechsel einer englischen Dame über Judenthum
und Semitismus. Stuttgart, 1883 (Levy und Müller). pp.
78.   **P.**

19. Christliche Zeugnisse gegen die Blutbeschuldigung der
Juden. Berlin, 1882 (Walther und Apolant). 8vo.
pp. 57.   **P.**
[Containing replies sent to Rabbi Lipschitz of Szanto from the
Theological Faculties of the Universities of Amsterdam, Copen-
hagen, Leyden, and Utrecht, from Catholic Bishops Kopp and
Reinkens, and from Profs. Delitzsch, Dillmann, Ebers, Fleischer,
De Lagarde, Müller, Nöldeke, Riehm, Stade, Strack, Wünsche.]

20. Les Conventions commerciales de la Roumanie devant
le droit public européen. Paris, 1878. 8vo. pp. 44.   **P.**

20a. Esther Solymosi, Der Prozess von Tisza-Eszlar.
Nebst den Portraits sämmtlicher Angeklagter, sowie der
Esther Solymosi und des Moritz Scharf und den Abbil-
dungen der Synagoge und Wohnung des Tempeldieners.
2te Auflage. Berlin, 1883 (M. Schulze).   **A.**

21. Ferdinand Lassalle und seine Stellung zum Judenthum. Magdeburg, 1879. [H. B. xx. 79.]   **P.**
[Aus "Israelitsche Wochenschrift."]

22. Die Fremdlinge in unserem Heime! Ein Mahnwort
an das deutsche Volk von einem Berliner Bürger. Berlin,
1877 (Niendorf). 8vo. pp. 52.   **A.**

23. Gebrauchen die Juden Christenblut? Eine Kultur-
historische Studie über die zahlreichen seitens der Juden
begangenen Opfermorde an Christen. Berlin (M.
Schulze). 1882. 12mo.   **A.**

24. Von der Geldmacht der Juden. Sonderabdruck aus
der "Israelit. Wochenschrift." Magdeburg, 1879. [H.
B. xx. 29.]   **P.**

25. Hepp! Hepp! Süsssaure Stöckerei in 1 Vorschrei
und 7 Gejohlen. Berlin, n.d. (Max Marcus). 8vo.
pp. 16.   **P.**
[With illustrated title-page, pigs.]

Anonymous—*continued.*

26. Herr Prof. Zöllner und das Judenthum. Magdeburg, 1879. [H. B. xx. 29.] **P.**
[Aus "Israelitische Wochenschrift."]

27. Hetz- und Brandschriften. Abdruck aus "Europa," No. 45, 1880. 8vo. pp. 3. **A.**

28. Die Hinrichtung des "Judenheiligen" Gotthold Ephraim Lessing durch Dr. Eduard Dühring in Berlin. Ein Echo aus dem Bregenzer Schriftstellerwinkel. Bregenz, 1881 (Wagner). 8vo. pp. 15. **P.**
[*Cf.* Dühring, No. 164.]

29. Israel und die Gojim. Beiträge zur Beurtheilung der Judenfrage. Leipzig, 1880 (Grunow). 8vo. pp. 316 and i. **A.**
[Answered by Schleinitz, No. 456.]

30. Juda's Ahnen-Saal, oder die jüdischen Gauner in Deutschland ; nach den amtlichen Ermittelungen des ehemaligen Kriminal-Aktuars Thiele in Berlin, 1841. Berlin, 1881 (Julius Ruppel). 12mo. pp. 109. **A.**

31. Der Juden Antheil am Verbrechen. Auf Grund der amtlichen Statistik über die Thätigkeit der Schwurgerichte in vergl. Darstellung mit den christlichen Confessionen. 2 Auflage. Berlin, 1881 (Otto Hentze). 8vo. pp. 19. **A.**
[Answered by Dr. S. Löwenfeldt, No. 285, q.v.; also reply in *Statist. Jahrbuch für Berlin*, 8. Jahrgang für 1880, pp. 237-9.]

32. Die Judenfrage. "Denkschrift" über die "Ursachen" eines erfolgten Uebertritts zur "christlichen" Kirche und die sich aus derselben, wie auf Grundlage vorherrschend spezifisch christlicher "Weltanschauung," ergebende "Veranlassung" für die "gebildeten" Deutschen (insb. "ungläubigen") Juden zur Ueberantwortung der künftigen Generation an die "christliche" Kirche. Von einem Offizier a. D. 1881. München (Franz). 8vo. pp. xii. and 98. **C.**
[Said to be by von Henle.]

33. Die Judenhetze in Russland und ihre Ursachen. Zugleich ein Mahnwort an Deutschland. Von einem Christen. Hamburg, 1882 (Christians und Schultheis). 8vo. pp. viii. and 32. **P.**
[With "Ein Brief an den Verfasser anstatt einer Vorrede."]

Anonymous—*continued.*

34. Die Juden im deutschen Staats- und Volksleben. Separatabdruck aus der "Deutschen Reichs-Post." Dritte Auflage. Frankfurt/a/M. 1878. 12mo. pp. 49. **A.**
[See Bankberger, No. 82.]

35. Die Juden in der Musik. (Separatabdruck aus "Die Deutsche Wacht.") Berlin, 1881 (O. Hentze.) 8vo. pp. 19. **A.**

36. Vom Judenthum im gesellschaftlichen Leben. Ein Beitrag zur Wucherfrage. Magdeburg, 1879. [H. B. xx. 29.] **P.**
[Aus d. "Israelit. Wochenschrift."]

37. Vom Judenthum im öffentlichen Leben und in der Presse. Magdeburg, 1879. [H. B. xx. 29.] **P.**
[Aus "Israelitische Wochenschrift."]

38. Die Juden und der deutsche Staat. Achte Auflage. Berlin, 1877 (M. A. Niendorf). 8vo. pp. 68. **A.**
[First published in 1862. Author Nordmann, see Naudh. No. 321.]

39. Die Judenverfolgungen in Russland. Zwei Berichte des Times-Correspondenten (Artikel vom 11. und 13. Januar 1882). Zum Besten der Verfolgten. Berlin, 1882 (Gerschel). 8vo. pp. 24. **P.**
[Translation of *Times* articles No. 52, omitting Map and Appendix.]

40. Die Juden von einem Christen. Berlin, 1877 (E. Grosser). 8vo. pp. 61. **P.**

41. Der jüdische Referendarius. 1875. **A.**
[For issuing this pamphlet the Editor of the *Schlesische Zeitung* was fined 100 Marks. *Cf.* following No.]

42. Der jüdische Referendarius in der Schlesischen Volkszeitung. Magdeburg, 1879. [H. B. xx. 29.] **P.**
[Aus "Israelit. Wochenschrift."]

43. Luther und die Juden. Den deutschen Studenten gewidmet von einem Commilitonen. Leipzig, 1881. (Frohberg). 12mo. pp. 32. **A.**

7

Anonymous—*continued.*

44. Manifest an die Regierungen u. Völker der durch das Judenthum gefährdeten christlichen Staaten. Chemnitz, 1882. 8vo. pp. 16. [H. B. xxi. 124.]   **A.**
[Said to have been composed by V. Istoczy as invitation to the Dresden Anti-Semitic Congress.]

45. Der Mauscheljude, von einem deutschen Advokaten. Ein Volksbüchlein für deutsche Christen aller Bekenntnisse. 3 Auflage. Paderborn, 1879. 8vo. pp. 39. [H. B. xxi. 51.]   **A.**

46. Neu-Palästina, oder das verjüdelte Deutschland. Ein milder Beitrag zur Kenntniss der Judenfrage im sogenannten "Deutschen" Reiche, von einem Konservativen. Berlin, 1879 (O. Hentze). 8vo. pp. 52.   **A.**

47. "Ob der Jude oder Christ, saget mir wer besser ist?" Historisch social-politische Betrachtungen über die Unbilligkeit und Unklugheit der antisemitischen Bestrebungen, von einem Ultramontanen. München, 1882 (F. Weinreich). 8vo. pp. 30.   **P.**

48. Offener Brief eines jüdischen Predigers an A. Stöcker. Leipzig, 1879. [H. B. xx. 30.]   **P.**

49. Offenes Sendschreiben an den Herrn Prof. Bluntschli. Magdeburg, 1879. [H. B. xx. 29.]   **P.**
[Aus "Israelit. Wochenschrift."]

50. Outrages upon the Jews in Russia. Report of the Public Meeting at the Mansion House on Wednesday, February 1st, 1882. With an Appendix containing lists of [42] towns where similar meetings were held, together with a letter addressed to the Chief Rabbi by the Graduates of Oxford University. Published by the Council of the Anglo-Jewish Association. 8vo. pp. 32.   **P.**
[Also translated into French and German.]

51. Persecution des Israélites en Russie. Paris. (Imp. veuve Zabieha.)   **P.**
[Broadsheets (yellow) issued by the Alliance Israélite of Paris (?), about 500 mm. by 350 mm. in 5 cols. containing translation from Russian and Polish journals in French. First series numbered with Arabic numerals, No. 1, April, 1881, to No. 50, July, 1882. Second series numbered with Roman numerals, No. 1, July, 1882, in progress.]

Anonymous—*continued.*

52. Persecution of the Jews in Russia, 1881. Reprinted from the *Times*, with Map and Appendix. London, 1882 (Spottiswoode). 8vo. pp. 31 and map.   P.

[Written by present compiler, pp. 1-13 appeared in *Times* of Jan. 11th; pp. 13-21 in that of Jan. 13th. Republished with "Map of Localities mentioned in this Pamphlet" and "Appendix: List of 167 places in Russia where Jews have been persecuted 1881." Two editions, each of 5000 copies, were distributed of this pamphlet during the agitation in England, Jan.-March, 1882. Translated into German, v. No. 39.]

The result of the *Times* report may be indicated by the following diary of newspaper articles on the subject :—

Jan. 11. *Pall Mall Gazette*, 2 notes.
 12. Ditto, letter, "D.F.S."
 14. *Spectator ; Saturday Review.*
 15. *Observer ; Lloyd's Weekly.*
 16. Letter of Lord Shaftesbury in *Times.*
 ,, Letter of Canon Farrar in *Morning Post.*
 ,, *St. James's Gazette.*
 17. Bishop of Oxford in *Times.*
 ,, *Daily News ; Morning Post.*
 18. *Standard ; Daily Telegraph.*
 ,, Letter of O. K. in *Times.* Leader.
 19. *Guardian ;* Rev. Dr. H. Adler in *Times.*
 21. *Tablet ; Spectator ; Saturday Review.*
 22. Requisition to Lord Mayor to summon Mansion House Meeting published in *Observer.*
 23. *Standard; Sheffield Independent; Glasgow News ; Morning Post ; Daily Telegraph.*
 24. *Daily News ; Morning Advertiser.*
 25. *Times ; Truth ; Pall Mall.*
 26. Letter of Myers in *Times.* [*cury.*
 27. *Daily News ; Daily Telegraph ; Liverpool Mer-*
 28. Answer to Consular Report in *Times,* I.; *Pall Mall ; Saturday Review.*
 30. Answer II. *Scotsman : Sheffield Independent ; Standard.*

Feb. 1. Letter from British Resident in Odessa, *Daily News ; Pall Mall ; Truth.*

Anonymous—*continued.*

Feb. 2. *Times; Morning Advertiser; Morning Post; Daily News; Standard; Daily Telegraph;* etc., commenting on Mansion House Meeting.
    4. *Spectator.*

53. Petition des citoyens suisses de confession israélite à la haute assemblée féderale de la confédération suisse au sujet de la ratification de la convention de commerce avec la Roumanie. Bâle, 1878. 8vo. pp. 16.   **P.**

53a. Der Process von Tisza-Eszlar, verhandelt in Nyíregyhaza im Jahre 1883. Eine genaue Darstellung der Anklage, der Zeugenverhöre, der Vertheidigung und des Urtheils. Nach authentischen Berichten bearbeitet, mit 20 Illustrationen. Wien, 1883 (A. Hartleben). 8vo. pp. 96.   **P.**

[Hartleben's *Chronik der Zeit.* 7tes Heft. Issued day after conclusion of trial.]

54. La Question Israélite en Roumanie par un Ancien Député. Paris, 1879 (Blot). 8vo. pp. 30.   **A.**

55. La Question Juive en Allemagne. Extrait du *Correspondant.* Paris, 1881 (Jules Gervais). 8vo. pp. 49. **P.**

55a. La Question Juive. Etude Historique. Lille, 1882 (Desclée). 8vo. pp. 92.   **P.**

56. Der reine Mosaismus. Interconfessionelle Religionslehre. II. Vom Verfasser der "Religion des kommenden Jahrhunderts." Budapesth (Aigner), 1882. 8vo. pp. 56.   **P.**

57. Russian Atrocities, 1881. Supplementary Statement issued by the Russo-Jewish Committee in confirmation of "The Times" Narrative. London, 1882. (Wertheimer, Lea, & Co.). 8vo. pp. 35.   **P.**

["Signed on behalf of the Russo-Jewish Committee, N. M. de Rothschild, Chairman."]
[In answer to Consular Reports *v.* Official Papers. England, Russia, No. 1, 1882.]
[Also translated into German. "Die Russischen Verfolgungen der Juden. Russische Greuel. Supplementarbericht."]

58. Die Russischen Verfolgungen. Fünfzehn Briefe aus Süd-Russland. Frankfurt/a/M., 1882. (J. Kauffmann). 8vo. pp. 61.   **P.**

[Translated from letters of Correspondent of *Jewish World.*]

Anonymous—*continued.*

59. Schleiden als Judengenosse.   Magdeburg, 1879.
[H.B. xx. 29.]   **P.**
[Aus "Israelit. Wochenschrift."]

60. Schuldig oder Nichtschuldig? Berlin, 1880. 8vo.
pp. 24. [H. B. xx. 79.]   **P.**

61. Semita in Aengsten. Authentisches Sendschreiben eines
polnischen Rabbiners an den Verfasser der "Sittenlehre
des Talmud und des zerstörenden Einflusses des Judenthums im deutschen Reiche.   Berlin, 1877. (M. A.
Niendorf.)   **A.**

62. Die Sittenlehre des Talmud und der zerstörende
Einfluss des Judenthums im deutschen Reich. 3 Auflage.
Berlin, 1876.   **A.**
[Abdruck aus der Deutschen Landeszeitung]

63. Socialpolitische Beiträge zur Judenfrage in Deutschland.   Aus dem practischen Leben der Provinz und
Grossstadt geschildert.

  Besser ein Character resignirt allein
  Als geopfert der Israélite-Alliance-Gemein.

Zweite Auflage. Berlin, n. d. (A. Klein). 8vo. pp. 44.
                                                      A.

63a. Eine Stimme aus dem Volke über die Judenfrage.
Offener Brief an Herrn Egon Waldigg. Cöln, 1880.
[H. B. xx. 33.]   **P.**

64. Die studentische Petition als Annex der allgemeinen
Petition, betreffend die Einschränkung der jüdischen
Machtstellung. Ein Beitrag zur Orientirung über Gründe
und Zwecke derselben. Leipzig, 1881. 8vo. pp. 40.
[H. B. xxi. 51.]   **A.**

65. Studien über die Judenfrage. Von einem Geächte-
ten. Erstes Heft. Ein öffentliches Geheimniss. Drittes
Heft. Aus dem classischen Lande des Wuchers. pp. 40.
Lemberg, 1880. (Seyfarth und Czajkowski.)   **A.**

66. Der Talmud, oder die Sittenlehre des Judenthums.
Nebst einem Anhang enthaltend Aussprüche deutscher
Geistesheroen, mit Portraits. Episoden über den zer-
störenden Einfluss des Judenthums. Statistisches, etc., etc.
Volksausgabe. Berlin, n. d. Schultze. 8vo. pp. 64. **A.**
[Statistics pp. 42-7.]

Anonymous—*continued.*

67. Th. Mommsen und sein Wort über unser Judenthum (Separat Abdruck aus "Die Deutsche Wacht"). Berlin, 1881 (O. Hentze). 8vo. pp. 8. **A.**

[Extract from "Deutsche Wacht." Cf. No. 311.]

68. Die Theorien des Herrn Hofprediger Stöcker in der Pastoral-Conferenz und die Frauen. Von einem Gläubigen im Evangelium des Friedens. Berlin, 1882 (Issleib). 8vo. pp. 68. **P.**

69. Votum eines Unbefangenen. Ein Beitrag zur Judenfrage von einem ehemaligen Liberalen. Berlin, 1881 (Heinicke). 8vo. pp. 36. **A.**

70. Die wahre Erlösung vom Antisemitismus. Von einem getauften Juden. Leipzig, 1883 (O. Wigand). 8vo. pp. 61. **C.**

71. Warum treten wir nicht in das Christenthum ein? Von einem Juden. Leipzig, 1882 (G. Wolf). 8vo. pp. 34. **P.**

72. Wir Juden. Betrachtungen und Vorschläge von einem Bukowinaer Juden. Zürich, 1883 (C. Schmidt). 8vo. pp. 30. **P.**

73. Ein Wort an Prof. Du Bois-Reymond. Magdeburg, 1879. **P.**

[Aus "Israelit. Wochenschrift," H.B. xx. 29.]

74. Ein Wort zur Judenfrage von einem ehemaligen Juden. Berlin, 1880 (Heinicke). 8vo. pp. 19. **C.**

75. Wucher und Intoleranz. Zugleich eine Antwort auf die Schrift von W. Marr : "Der Sieg des Judenthums über das Germanenthum" Von einem Unpartheiischen. Zürich, 1879 (Schabelitz). 12mo. pp. 36. **P.**

76. Zeitgedichte aus der "Wahrheit." Berlin, 1881 (M. Schutze). 8vo. pp. iv. and 135. **A.**

[Containing 52 "Lieder," etc.]

Austriacus [pseudonym].

77. Oesterreich ein Juwel in jüdischer Fassung. Juden-
wirthschaft und Judenherrschaft in Oesterreich-Ungarn.
Berlin, 1880 (O. Hentze). 8vo. pp. 42. **A.**

78. Wählet keinen Juden! Ein Mahn- und Warnungsruf
an die Völker Oesterreich-Ungarns. Berlin, 1881 (O.
Hentze). 8vo. pp. 35. **A.**

Avé-Lallermant.

79. Der Magnetismus als Beitrag zum Deutschen Gauner-
thum. Berlin, 1882. **P.**

[p. 19 occurs a strong protest against the Antisemitic movement
as a "mittelalterliche Reaction." Of importance, as the Anti-
semitics are perpetually quoting the author's "Deutsches Gauner-
thum" against the Jews.]

Backhaus, S.

80. Die Germanen ein semitischer Volksstamm. Geschicht-
licher und Sprachlicher Nachweis. Berlin, Duessner
(Dec. 1878). 8vo. pp. 57. **P.**
[German version of "Anglo-Israel" craze.]

Bamberger, Ludwig.

81. Deutschthum und Judenthum. Separatabdruck aus
"Unsere Zeit": Deutsche Revue der Gegenwart. 2te
Auflage. Leipzig, (Brockhaus) 1880. 8vo. pp. vi.+38.
P.

Bankberger, Dr. Hilarius [? pseudonym].

82. Die Juden im deutschen Staats- und Volksleben.
Vierte erheblich vermehrte und verbesserte Auflage.
Frankfurt a/M., 1879. (Separat-Abdruck aus der
"Deutschen Reichs-Post.") 12mo. pp. 114. **A.**
[First published anonymously, cf. No. 34. Giving bibliographical
list, pp. 98-112.]

83. Die sogenannte Deutsche "Reichsbank," eine privi-
ligirte Actien-Gesellschaft von und für Juden. Nebst
Betrachtungen über Lasker'hafte und Bamberger'liche
Politik. Berlin, 1876 (Niendorf). 8vo. pp. 92. **A.**

Barine, Arvide [pseudonym].

84. Le juif Russe jugé par lui-même. In *Revue politique*,
10 June, 1882. **A.**

Basily, C. M.

84a. Rapport sur la question Juive présenté au Zemstvo d'Odessa. Odessa, 1881. **A.**

[Referred to in the *Edinburgh Review*, April, 1883.]

Bassin, Elieser [Schottischer Missionsprediger].

85. Die Judenfrage und die zu ihrer Lösung vorgeschlagenen Mittel. Angeregt und herausgegeben von E. B. Erstes Heft. Jasii [Jassy, Rumania], 1881 (Gheorghia). 8vo. pp. 40+1. **P.**

[Containing "Antwort des Herrn Folticirano," pp. 12-32, on statistics, etc., of Jews in Rumania.]

Baumgarten, M. [Prof. der Theologie.]

86. Stöcker's gefälschtes Christenthum. Rede gehalten am 15. October 1881 in Berlin. Berlin, 1881 (Stuhr). 8vo. pp. 33. **P.**

87. Wider Herrn Hofprediger Stöcker. Eine christliche Stimme über die Judenfrage. Berlin, 1881 (Stuhr). 8vo. pp. 25. **P.**

Beck, Dr. C. L.

88. Eine Rechtfertigung der Juden und wahre Lösung der Judenfrage. Leipzig, 1881 (Morgenstern). 8vo. pp. iv.+105. **P.**

Berliner, Dr. A.

89. Persönliche Beziehungen zwischen Christen und Juden im Mittelalter. Halberstadt, 1882 (Meyer). 8vo. pp. 29. **P.**

Bernstein, Dr. A.

90. Herrn Stöcker's Treiben und. Lehren. Berlin, n.d. (Verlag. d. Volksztg, Schilke). Separat-Abdruck aus der "Volkszeitung." 8vo. pp. 27. **P.**

Berthold, Ludwig.

91. Cassel! Predige Deinen Juden und Dir selbst! Ein Mahnwort an Herrn Judenmissionär Professor Dr. Paulus Cassel und dessen Stammesgenossen. Berlin, 1881 (Luckhardt). 8vo. pp. 34. **A.**

[Cf. Cassel Nos. 128-133.]

Beta, O. [pseudonym].

92. Darwin, Deutschland und die Juden, oder Juda-Jesuitismus. Dreiunddreissig Thesen nebst einer Nachschrift über einen vergessenen Factor der Volkswirthschaft. Sr. Durchlaucht dem Fürsten Bismarck in Ehrfurcht gewidmet. Zweite Auflage. Berlin, 1876. Selbstverlag. Expedition der Eisenbahn-Zeitung. 8vo. pp. 48. **A.**

Bey, Major Osman.

93. Die Eroberung der Welt durch die Juden. 7te Auflage. Wiesbaden, 1875; also English Translation : The Conquest of the World by the Jews. An Historical and Ethnical Essay. By Major Osman Bey, Author of "La Turquie sous le régne d'Abdul Aziz." Revised and Translated by F. W. Mathias. St. Louis (U.S.A.) : 1878. Paper, pp. 71. **A.**

Bloch, J. S.

94. Contro l'Anti-Semitismo. Confutazione del Dr. J. S. Bloch. Versione italiana edita da G. Zerkowitz. Trieste 1883 (Amati). 8vo. pp. 74. **P.**
[Translations of Nos. 96 and 97.]

95. Gegen die Anti-Semiten. Eine Streitschrift. Wien, 1882 (Löwy). 8vo. pp. 39. **P.**

96. Des K. K. Prof. Rohling neueste Fälschungen. Separat-Abdruck aus der "Wiener Allgemeinen Zeitung" vom 6 Jan. 1883. Wien, 1883. 8vo. pp. 31. **P.**

97. Prof. Rohling und das Wiener Rabbinat oder "Der arge Schalmerei." Separat-Abdruck aus der "Wiener Allgemeinen Zeitung," vom 22. Dec. 1882. Wien, 1882. Selbstverlag. 8vo. pp. 29. **P.**

Bloch, Philipp.

98. Prof. Rohling's Falschmünzerei auf talmudischem Gebiete. Posen, 1876 (Merzbach). 8vo. pp. 31. **P.**

Bluntschli, Prof. Dr.

99. Der Staat Rumänien und das Rechtsverhältniss der Juden in Rumänien. Berlin, 1879. 8vo. pp. 27. **P.**

Bluntschli, Prof. Dr.—*continued.*

100. Roumania and the Legal Status of the Jews in Roumania. An Exposition of Public Law. Translated from the German with the sanction of the author. Issued by the Anglo-Jewish Association. 1879. 8vo. pp. 31. **P.**

[There is also a French translation issued by the *Alliance Israélite.*]

Bodek, Arn.

101. Hat das Judenthum dem Wucherwesen Vorschub geleistet? Flugblatt herausg. vom Israelitischen Gemeindebunde. Leipzig, 1879. 8vo. pp. 17. [H.B. xix. 52.] **P.**

Börne, Dr. Ludwig.

102. Offenes Sendschreiben über die Juden von Löb Baruch an den deutschen Reichstagabgeordneten und Heidelberger Professor Dr. H. G. von Treitschke. Berlin, 1880, pp. 20. **P.**

Bothmer, Countess M. von [Author of " German Home Life."]

103. Aut Cæsar aut Nihil [a Novel]. London, 1883 (Longmans). 8vo. 3 vols. **P.**

[Of interest as containing sympathetic views on Russian Jews, although the authoress had previously written against the Jews. *Cf.* Periodicals—England—London—*Contemporary Review.*]

Bourdeau, J.

104. Les Allemands vaincus par les Juifs im *Journal des Débats*, 5. Nov., 1879. Cf. *Le Temps*, 1 and 13 Jan., 1880. **P.**

Brake, Georg [Pfarrer in Oldenburg].

105. Zur deutschen Judenfrage. Gotha (F. A. Perthes), 1880. 8vo. pp. 100. **A.**

Braphmann, Jac. [Convert in the pay of the Russian Government.]

106. Das Buch Kahala. Materialien zur Erforschung des jüd, Lebensischen gesammelt und übersetzt [Russian]. St.

Braphman, Jac.—*continued.*

Petersburg, 1869—75. Two Volumes. 8vo. pp. viii. and 158, and iii. and 479. [H. B. xviii. 84.] **A.**

[Answered by Serberling No. 473, excerpted by Ragozin, No. 404. This work as well as a French translation, *Le Livre de Kabal,* Paris, 1874, has been withdrawn from circulation.]

Bresslau, Prof. Harry.

107. Zur Judenfrage. Sendschreiben an Herrn. Prof. Dr. Heinrich von Treitschke. Zweite, mit einem Nachwort vermehrte Auflage. Berlin (Dümmler), 1880. 8vo. pp. 31. **P.**

Broadsheets.

108. Antisemitische Flugblätter. Berlin, 1879, 1880. Folio. [H. B. xx. 30.] **A.**

    1. Israel an allen Orten. ["Deutsche Wacht."]
    2. Hr. Prof. Lazarus und die jüdischen Deutschen.
    3. Die Mässigkeitsjuden.
    4. Israelitische Mosaik. ["Deutsche Wacht."]
    5. Wie sich einmal . . . . ein Prediger über die Juden ausliess ["Deutsche Reform."]

109. "Das Comité der Antifortschrittlichen Vereinigung im Ersten Reichstagswahlkreis," mentions that its candidate is Herr Liebermann von Sonnenberg, invites to various meetings, but "allen Juden ist der Besuch unserer Versammlung untersagt." **A.**

110. Issued by "Das Conservative Central-Comité," recommending various candidates for the 7 Electoral Districts of Berlin, and on 4th page "Unser Kandidat für den II. Reichstags-Wahlkreis." (Hofprediger Stöcker). With Portrait and Biography. 4to. pp. 4. **A.** [Printed by Behr.]

111. Deutsche Mitbürger! Der Quartalwechsel steht vor der Thür. Wollt Ihr noch länger unsere Feinde mit dem Lohne eurer redlichen Arbeit unterstützen? *Schafft die Judenblätter ab!*

Für die Interessen des Judenthums schreiben:—
Berliner Tageblatt, National-Zeitung, Tribüne, Vossische Zeitung, Volkszeitung, Berliner Zeitung, Montags-Zeitung, Börsen-Courier, Berliner Börsen-Zeitung, Kladderadatsch, Ulk, Wespen.

Broadsheets—*continued.*

Unabhängig von Jüdischem Einfluss sind :—*Der Reichs-bote, Die Post, Staatsbürger Zeitung, Norddeutsche Allgemeine Zeitung, Deutsches Tageblatt, Neue Preussische (Kreuz) Zeitung, Berliner Fremdenblatt, Germania (Catholisch), Neue Börsen Zeitung, Das Schwarze Blatt, Die Wahrheit, Schalk, Fleigende Blätter, Der Staat, Socialist, Berliner Ostend Zeitung, Der Hallesche Thorbote. Patriotische Zeitung (Liegnitz), Deutsche Reform (Dresden)s Deutsche Wacht*⎫ *Monätlich.*
Kulturkämpfer⎭

Und nun gehe direct nach Haus mit diesem Zettel, Deutscher Zeitungsleser : und mache Dich sofort daran Deine bisher gehaltene *Judenzeitung* abzubestellen damit nicht fernerhin noch Dein Haus, Deine dir heiligste Familie vergiftet wird durch *Judenlectüre.*   **A.**

112.   Same as preceding, omitting end and adding follow-ing newspapers and periodicals :— PROSEMITIC—*Berliner Nachrichten, Deutsche Rundschau* (Julius Levy *genannt* Rodenberg), *Gegenwart* und *Nord und Süd* (Paul Lindau), *Kölnische Zeitung, Hartungsche Zeitung* (Königsberg), *Magdeburger Zeitung, Weser Zeitung, Gartenlaube* (Leipzig). ANTISEMITIC —*Apollo, Schlesische Zeitung* (Breslau), *Saale Zeitung* (Halle), *Norddeutsche Presse* (Neustettin), *Mecklenburgische Zeitung, Daheim.*   **A.**

113.   Deutsche Mitbürger Berlins ! / Wähler des I. Reichs-tagswahlkreises ! . . . . und nun entscheide sich Jeder / Hier der Candidat der Juden und Judengenossen, der reiche Gründer und Manchestermann, der Jude Ludwig Löwe und dort ihm gegenüber / der Candidat des deutschen, christlichen Glaubens, der Anhänger der socialen Reform des Fürsten Bismarck / Herr Max Liebermann von Sonnenberg. / . Berlin den 21 October, 1881). / Das Komité der antifortschrittlichen Vereinigung im I. Reichstagswahlkreise.   (Starcke, Printer)   **A.**

114.   Deutscher Reform Verein zu Berlin / Donnerstag den 22 Juni—Abends 8 Uhr). / Oeffentliche Versamm-lung im Sommers-Salon, Potsdammerstrasse, 9. / Vor-trag des Herrn W. Pickenbuch / über / "Was will die

18

Broadsheets—*continued.*

Deutsche Reformpartei und wie stellt / sich dieselbe zur
Judenfrage. / Jüdisches Publicum ist ausgeschlossen
. . . . Kleines Eintrittsgeld nach Belieben. (Printer,
Julius Ruppel). **A.**

115. Deutsche Mitbürger ! . . . . Quotes article from
"Berliner Börsen-Courier" (Redacteure: Gebrüder
Davidsohn) of 3 August, 1881, on the "Kyffhäuser-
Fest unserer studirenden Söhne und Brüder" in which
the question is asked, "Kann man sich ein hässlicheres
Gemisch von Streberthum, Pseudo-Enthusiasmus, Be-
trunkenheit und Duckmäuserei denken als es in dieser
sogenannten "studentischen" Bewegung zu Tage tritt?"
The quotation is issued by the "Anti-Semitische Liga"
of Berlin, Aug., 1881. **A.**

116. Extra-Blatt über den Christenmord in Ungarn—Die
Synagoge von Tissa-Esslar (Illustration)—Die gericht-
liche Anklage der Mörder. (Printer, Julius Ruppel).
Newspaper, 4to. **A.**

117. Flugblätter der christl. socialen Arbeiterpartie.
(From the *Christlich Socialich. Kalender für* 1882.
H.B. xxi. 28 and 49. Cf. No. 123.) **A.**

   13. Unsere Forderungen an das moderne Judenthum.
   14. Nothwehr gegen das moderne Judenthum.
   15. Die schlechte Presse.
   16. Die wahre Toleranz.
   17. Die Selbstvertheidigung des modernen Juden-
       thums in dem Geisteskampf der Gegenwart.
   18. Das Judenthum, der Fortschritt und das Volks-
       schulwesen in Berlin.
   19. König Hiskias, die Volksschule und der Ber-
       liner Fortschritt.
   21. Der Kern der Judenfrage.
   22. Ist die Bibel Wahrheit?
   23. Die Gegner der christlich-socialen Bewegung.
   25. Der Kampf des Lichts gegen die Finsterniss,
       der Character und die Aufgabe der Gegenwart.
   26. Der Eid.

Broadsheets—*continued.*

> 27. Das unzweifelhaft Berechtigte, Edle und Noth-
> wendige der gegenwärtigen antijüdischen
> Bewegung.
> 28. Das Aufwachen der deutschen Jugend.
> 29. Principien, Thatsachen und Ziele in der Juden-
> frage.

118. Zur Erinnnerung an das Deutsche National Volksfest
veranstaltet vom Conservativen Central-Comité am 2 Sept.
1881. Folio, pp. 4. **A.**

[On 4th page Germany riding on a winged horse with a banner
"Mit Gott für Kaiser und Reich" and trampling on "graue
Internationale" (= Catholics) " goldene Internationale " (= Jews)
"rothe Internationale " (= Socialists).]

119. Erster Berliner Reichswahlkreis. Mitbürger ! . . .
Appeal to elect Ludwig Löwe on Oct. 21. Issued by a
Liberal " Verein," referring to Liebermann as " Vorsit-
zender derjeniger Versammlungen gewesen ist in welchen
nach Stöckerschen Recepten—nur diesen überbietend—
Judenhetze getrieben wurde." (Printer, A. Haack.) **P.**

120. Was wollen wir ? ending with " Fort mit der ver-
judeten Berliner Fortschrittspartei !" Berlin, Aug. 1881.
Der Vorstand des deutschen Volksvereins. 4to. pp. 2.
(Starcke, Printer.) **A.**

Brouner, Marco.

121. Les conventions commerciales et la constitution
roumaine. Bucharest, 12 Février (? 1879). 4to. pp. 4.
(H.B. xix. 125). **A.**

121a. Lettre addressée par la voie de la presse a l'illustre
Sénateur Marquis de Pepoli. Berlin, 1879. 4to. pp. 2.
[*Ibid.*] **A.**

Brüggen, Ernst v. d.

122. Russland und die Juden. Kulturgeschichtliche
Studien. Leipsic, 1882. (Veit.) pp. iv. and 100. **A.**

Calendar.

123. Der christlich-sociale Kalender für das Jahr 1882. Dritter Jahrgang. (Berlin, Wiegandt und Grieber.) **A.**

[pp. 51-3. *Deutschland und das Judenthum.* Eine Parabel von Karl Julius Müller (in verse).]

124. Kehraus ! Humoristisch-Satirischer Volkskalender der Wahrheit für das Jahr 1883. Berlin, 1882. (M. Schulze). 8vo. pp. 96. (With 60 Illustrations and History of Antisemitic Movement, and Portraits of Leaders, pp. 33-52.) **A.**

[The second issue for 1884 has now appeared.]

Campbell, Bartlett.

125. Siberia. A Drama. **P.**

[Dealing with the Jewish Question in Russia ; performed at San Francisco.—*Jewish Messenger*, 8 Dec. 1882.]

Canini, M. A.

125a. Gli Israeliti in Rumania e il commendatore B. E. Maineri, celebre antisemita. 2ª ediz. Venezia, 1883 (Fentana). 8vo. pp. 16. **P.**

126. La verita sulla questione degli Israeliti in Rumania. Rome, 1879. [From "Nuova Antologia," Aug. 1 and 15, 1879.] **P.**

Cards. [To be sent in letters, or pasted upon doors, etc.] v. Post-Cards, 388.

127. 1. Jude lass die Jungfer los !
   2. Judenknecht !
   3. Juden raus !
   4. Wählt keinen Juden.
   5. Juden raus ! ["death's head and cross bones "].
   6. Die strafende Hand der Nemesis, L.L. Zur Züchtigung für Unverschämte. **A.**

[Cf. Advertisements. No. 5.]

Cassel, Prof. Paulus (Prediger an der Christus Kirche).

Cf. Berthold, No. 91.]
128. Die Antisemiten und die Evangelische Kirche.

Cassel, Prof. Paulus— *continued.*

Sendschreiben an einen evangelischen Geistlichen von
Prof. P. C. Berlin, 1881 (Wohlgemuth.) 8vo. pp. 46.
P.

129. Christliche Sittenlehre. Eine Auslegung des Briefes
Pauli an Titus. Mit einer Schlussbemerkung über
Semitismus. Zur Erinnerung an den 28 Mai, 1855.
Zweite Auflage. Berlin, 1880. (Stahr.) 8vo. pp. 112.
P.

130. Der Judengott und Richard Wagner. Eine Antwort
an die *Bayreuther Blätter* zum 28 Mai, 1881. Berlin,
1881. (Wohlgemuth). 8vo. pp. 44. P.

131. Die Juden in der Weltgeschichte. Berlin, 1880
(Gerschel). 8vo. pp. 30. P.

132. Ueber die Abstammung der englischen Nation.
Berlin, 1880. (Herbig). 8vo. pp. iv. and 55—81. P.

133. Wider Heinrich von Treitschke. Für die Juden.
Berlin, 1880 (Stahn). 12mo. pp. 28. P.

Castelar, Emilio.

134. Article in 'Elvin.' Translated into German and
read before the Literary Congress at Vienna. 15th Sept.
1881. P.

Chevalier (pseudonym).

135. Börsen-Silhouetten. (Besonderer Abdruck aus dem
"Börsen-Wochenblatt.") Berlin, 1880 (W. H. Kühl).
8vo. pp. i. and 52. A.
[Typical characters on Berlin Bourse, among others VIII. Peter
Schlemiel, 23, and the Schnorrer, XVI. p. 50.]

Christlieb, A.

136. Was uns in der Religion Noth thut. Ein Weckruf
auf die Bekenner Jesu und die Bekenner Mose. Berlin,
1879. 8vo. pp. 51. H.B. xx. 30. C.

Chwolson, Prof. D. A.

137. Gebrauchen die Juden Christenblut? Eine Untersuchung (in Russian). 2e· Aufl. St. Petersburg, 1879.
8vo. pp. 69. P.
[Extract from a larger work on same subject, a second edition of
which, pp. xvi.—386, appeared in Russian, St. Petersburg, 1880.]

Cleef, Isidore van.

137a. Juifs et Chrétiens. Deuxième édition avec une lettre de M. E. Renan. Bruxelles, 1883 (Lebègue). 8vo. pp. viii. and 40. **P.**

[Renan's letter, merely formal acknowledgment.]

Cobbe, Frances Power.

138. Progressive Judaism (in *Contemporary Review*), Nov. 1882. **P.**

[Welcoming and discussing article of Montefiore, No. 312.]

Coën, A.

139. A proposita dell' agitazione anti-semitica in Germania. In *Rivista Europea*, Nuova Serie. Anno XII. 16 March, 1881, pp. 888—897. **P.**

Cohen, Dr. Hermann.

140. Ein Bekenntniss in der Judenfrage. Berlin, 1880 (Dümmler). 8vo. pp. 25. **P.**

[Replying to Treitschke, No. 506, but opposing Lazarus, No. 274.]

Cohn, E.

141. Zwei Erwiderungs-Vortraege gehalten in den Versammlungen der Christlich-socialen Arbeiterpartei am 19 September u. 10 October, 1879, von E.C. gegen den Hof- u. Domprediger A. Stöcker über das Thema: "Unsere Forderungen an das moderne Judenthum." Berlin, 1879 (Selbstverlag). 12mo. pp. 20. **P.**

Comptes-rendus.

142. Hebrew Emigrants' Aid Society of New York. Reports of the President and Treasurer for 1882 (New York, Executive Offices, 15, State Street.) 8vo. pp. 19, and Table of Accounts. **P.**

143. Persecution of the Jews in Russia. Mansion House Relief Fund. Liverpool Commission. (Reports and Accounts). Liverpool, 1882 (Egerton Smith). 8vo. pp. 14. **P.**

144. Sottoscrizione a favore degli Israeliti Russi. Livorno, 1881 (Published by the Leghorn Committee). **P.**

Comptes-rendus—*continued*.

145. Rechenschaftsbericht des Hilfscomités zur Unterstützung der verunglückten Israeliten während der im Jahre 1881 stattgehabten Unruhen. Kiew, 1882. (Perlis.) 8vo. pp. 52, and 2 Tables. **P.**

[Also published in French, *Compte-rendu du Comité de secours.*]

Cox, Hon. S. Samuel.

146. Russo-Jewish Question. Speech delivered in the House of Representatives July 31, 1882, on the Persecution of the Jews in Russia. 8vo. pp. 25, and Map. **P.**

[pp. 20-25 giving Appendix of " Russian Persecutions of Jews, 1881, No. 52, and Map from same.]

Crezzulesco, Emmanuel (Ancien agent diplomatique de Roumanie à Paris).

147. Les Israélites en Roumanie. Paris, 1879 (Dentu). 8vo. pp. 60. **A.**

Cunow, L. (Redacteur).

148. Die Gemeingefährlichkeit des jüdischen Einflusses. Vortrag gehalten am 19 Mai, 1882, zu Berlin. 8vo. pp. 8. **A.**

Daab, H.

149. Der Thalmud in Vortraegen. Leipzig, 1883 (1882) (Böhme). 8vo. pp. ii. and 204. **A.**

[Zur Judenfrage, pp. 189-204.]

Darmesteter, James.

150. Un coup d'œil sur l'histoire du peuple juif. Paris, 1881 (Lib. Nouvelle). 8vo. pp. 21. **P.**

[English Translation in *Hebrew Review.* No. 6. Republished in his *Etudes Orientales*, Paris, 1883. Translated into German, Hungarian, and Roumanian.]

Davis, Israel, M.A.

151. The Jews in Roumania. 2nd Edition. 1872. **P.**

Delitzsch, Prof. Franz.

152. Christenthum und jüdische Presse. Selbsterlebtes. Erlangen, 1882 (Deichert). 8vo. pp. 69. **A.**

Delitzsch—*continued.*

153. Was Dr. Aug. Rohling beschworen hat und be-
schwören will. Zweite Streitschrift in Sachen des Antisemitismus. Leipsic, 1883 (Dörffling und Franke). **P.**
[In reference to Rohling, 437.]

154. Rohling's Talmudjude beleuchtet von F. D. 5ᵗᵉ
Aufl. 1881. Leipzig (Dörffling und Franke). 8vo. pp.
86. **P.**
[Against Rohling, 436. Answered by same, 435.]

154a. Schachmatt den Blutlügnern Rohling und Justus.
Erlangen, 1883 (Deichert). 8vo. pp. 43. **P.**

154b. Neueste Traumgeschichte der antisemitischen Pro-
pheten. Sendschreiben an Prof. Zöckler in Greifswald.
Erlangen, 1883 (Deichert). 8vo. pp. 32.
[Cf. Justus, No. 251a, and Rohling, No. 437a.]

Dessauer, Dr. M.

155. Blüthen und Knospen der Humanität aus der Zeit
von Reuchlin bis Lessing, 1881. **P.**

Dictionary.

156. Kleiner Woerterschatz der englischen Sprache.
Berlin, 1882. (Issued by the Russian Refugees Committee of Berlin for refugees proceeding to America.)
12mo.

Diehle, August.

157. Die Antisemiten. Trauerspiel. München, 1881.
(Principal Character: Dr. Gottlieb Stock=Stöcker.) **A.**

Directory.

158. Adressbuch christlicher Firmen Berlins. Berlin
(Schulze.) (Dec. 1881.) 16mo. pp. 42. **A.**
[2 columns, about 25 addresses to a column.]

Döllinger, Dr. J. von.

159. The Jews in Europe. Address delivered at the
Meeting of the Royal Academy of Sciences at München on
July 25, 1881, by its President, J. v. D.. Translated from
the German, by special permission of the Ven. and Very
Rev. Author, by Dr. David Asher. Reprinted from the
Jewish Chronicle. London, 1881 (A. I. Myers). 8vo.
pp. 20. **P.**

Donath, Endre.

159a. Solymosi Eszter Legujabl tarsadalami regeny ket
kötelben. 1 köt. 1 füzet. Klausenburg, 1883 (K.) 8vo.
pp. 32. **A.**
[E. S. the latest social Romance, in 2 vols. First vol. first part.]

Donner, Friedr.

160. Das Judenthum in den Vereinigten Staaten von
Nord-Amerika. Eine Bekehrungschrift für die HH.
Pastoren Stöcker, Henrici, sowie für alle Judenhetzer.
Wien, 1881. [H. B. xxi. 48.] **P.**

Dreydorff, G.

161. Die Hofpredigerpartei und die Juden unter Landgraf
Phillip von Hessen. In *Protest. Kirchenzeitung*, 1880,
p. 570. **A.**

Dühring, Dr. E.

162. Der Ersatz der Religion durch Vollkommeneres,
die Ausscheidung alles Judenthums durch den modernen
Volkesgeist. Leipsic, 1883 (Reuther). 8vo. pp. iv.
and 268. **A.**

163. Die Judenfrage als Racen-, Sitten-, und Culturfrage
mit einer weltgeschichtlichen Antwort. Zweite verbesserte Auflage. Karlsruhe und Leipzig, 1881 (H.
Reuther). 8vo. pp. vi. and 161. **A.**
[With autograph signature of the author.]

164. Die Ueberschätzung Lessings und dessen Anwalt-
schaft für die Juden. Karlsruhe und Leipzig, 1881 (H.
Reuther). 8vo. pp. vi. and 93. **A.**
[With autograph signature.]

Duschak, Dr. M.

165. Die Moral der Evangelien und des Talmud. Eine
vergleichende Studie im Geiste unserer Zeit. Brünn,
1877 (Epstein). 8vo. pp. x. and 58. **P.**

166. *Tor Esther.* Mittel gegen die falschen Blutbeschuldigungen, nebst einem Anhange : Zur Sage und
Geschichte Polens. Krakau, 1883 (Selbstverlag). 8vo.
pp. 66. **P.**

Eisler, Dr. M.

167. Die Judenfrage in Deutschland. New York, 1880
(Selbstverlag.) (Hamburg, Nestler und Melle). 8vo.
pp. 94. **P.**

Eliot, George (Mary Ann Cross, *née* Evans).

168. Impressions of Theophrastus Such, 1879. London,
Blackwoods. XVIII. The Modern Hep! Hep! Hep!
pp. 313-357. **P.**

[Probably dealing with the attack of Goldwin Smith, Cf. pp.
335-6. German translation by E. Lehmann: *Das moderne Hep!
Hep! Hep! Die Juden und ihre Gegner*, Hamburg, 1880. 8vo.
pp. 39. Cf. Daniel Deronda, ch. xlii. pp. 388-405.]

Ellenberger, Heinrich.

169. Chronologische Reihenfolge der heiligen jüdischen
Tradition . . . . nebst einem Schlussworte an Prof. Dr.
Aug. Rohling. Buda-Pesth, 1883. 8vo. pp. 61. **P.**

[Answer to Rohling, pp. 48—56.]

170. Die Leiden und Verfolgungen der Juden und ihrer
Beschützer in chronologischer Reihenfolge. Budapest,
1882 (Zilahy). 8vo. pp. xvi. and 141, and 10 of
Index. **P.**

Endner, Wilhelm.

171. Zur Judenfrage. Offene Antwort auf das offene
Sendschreiben des Herrn Dr. Harry Bresslau an Herrn
von Treitschke. Berlin, 1882 (S. Hahne). 8vo. pp.
27. **A.**

Enodatus (pseudonym).

172. Juden und Judenhetze. Löbau, 1879. 8vo. pp.
33. [H.B. xx. 30.] **P.**

Erichson, A.

172a. Offener Brief an die Anti-Semiten. Berlin im
Nov. 1880. Auszug aus einem demnächst erscheinenden
grösseren Werke des Verfassers. (Liebrecht). 12mo.
pp. 7. **P.**

[In verse.]

Ernst, W. von.

173. Noch etwas vom besiegten Germanenthum. Offener Brief an die Herren Marr, Perinhart, v. Linden, Reymond, Sailer, Waldeg, etc. Dresden, 1879 (Grumbkow). 12mo. pp. 23. **A.**

Farkas, Ödön.

173a. A Zsidókérdés Magyarorszagon. Budapesth, 1881 (K.) 8vo. pp. 56. **P.**
[The Jewish Question in Hungary.]

Fastigato, Enrique Serrano.

173b. Estudios sociales y politicos. Madrid, 1881. **P.**
[With an essay "La Cruzada Europea contra los Judios."]

Fischer, Karl.

174. Gutmeinung über den Talmud der Hebräer. Verfasst von K. F., Zensor. Revisor und Translator im hebräischen Fache zu Prag. (Nach einem Manuscript vom Jahre 1802.) Wien, 1883 (Hölder). 8vo. pp. vi. and 112. **P.**

Fischer, Prof. Dr. Karl.

175. Antisemiten und Gymnasiallehrer: Ein Protest. Berlin, 1881 (Dümmler) 8vo. pp. 40. **P.**
[Against Siecke, No. 474.]

176. Heinrich v. Treitschke und sein Wort über unser Judenthum. Ein Wort zur Verständigung. Leipzig, 1880 (Schellmann). 8vo. pp. 40. **P.**

Fraenkel, Emanuel.

177. Erinnerung auf die von Prof. Dr. August Rohling verfasste Schrift: "Der Talmudjude." Dazu als Anhang: Ein Schreiben des Dr. Phil. Mansch an den Verfasser. Lemberg, 1874. (Rohatiner.) 8vo. pp. 52. **P.**
[Translated into Polish by N. Landa, 1876.]

Fraenkel, J.

178. La question juive. Paris, 1883 (Dentu.) 18mo. pp. 128. **P.**

Fraenkl, Dr. P. F.

179. Alle Israeliten sind Bürger für einander. Berlin,
1881. 8vo. pp. 12 (H. B. xxi. 49). **P.**

[Sermon, issued by request.]

Frantz, Constantin. [Cf. No. 210.]

180. Der Nationalliberalismus und die Judenherrschaft.
München, 1874 (Dr. M. Hattler). 8vo. pp. 64. **A.**

Freimann, Abr.

181. *Chésed Labraham.* Betrachtungen über den Juden-
krawall in Kiew. Berlin, 1880. 32. pp. 11. [St. H.
B. xxi. 53.] **P.**

[Der Reinertrag ist zur Verheirathung der Tochter des Dichters
bestimmt, der so beginnt,
" Im Jahre 1881 hat getroffen, In Kiew ein grosser Schreck
Das wollte, stark besoffen, Die Juden bringen um die Eck."
—*Steins.*]

Fremantle, Hon. and Rev. W. H.

182. The Future of Judaism in *Contemporary Review*,
July, 1878, pp. 773-789. **P.**

Freund, Dr. Leopold.

182a. Texte und Glossen : Resultate critischer Gänge
durch politische und nicht politische Gebiete mit
besonderer Rücksicht auf social-psychologischen Phä-
nomenen. Zurich, 1881 (Verlagsmagazin). **P.**

Frey, Thomas.

182b. Brennende Fragen. Erste Serie. Berlin, 1883
(M. Schulze). **A.**

182c. Leuchtkugeln. Alt-deutsch-antisemitische Kern-
sprüche. Berlin, 1883 (Schulze). **A.**

Friedeberg, M.

183. Practisches Judenthum. Ein Wort zur Verständigung, insbesondere an seine Glaubensgenossen gerichtet.
Leipzig, 1881 (K. Friese). 8vo. pp. 58. **P.**

Friedländer, M.

184. Fünf Wochen in Brody unter jüdisch-russischen Emigranten. Ein Beitrag zur Geschichte der russischen Judenverfolgung. Wien, 1882 (Waizner). 8vo. pp. 50.
                                                                                    P.

Förster, Dr. Bernhard.

185. Das Verhältniss des modernen Judenthums zur deutschen Kunst. Vortrag gehalten im Berliner Zweigverein des Bayreuther Patronats-Vereins. Berlin, (1881) (Schutze). 8vo. pp. iii. and 59.   **A.**

Franck, A. (Membre de l'Institut).

186. In *Annales de Philosophie Chrétienne*, October, 1882.   **P.**

Gauvain, Hermann.

187. Zur Judenfrage. Zwei Sendschreiben. Berlin and Leipzig, 1881 (Bidder). 8vo. pp. v. and 77.   **A.**

Gellion-Danglar, E.

188. Les Sémites et le Sémitisme au point de vue ethnographique, réligieux et politique. Paris, 1882 (Maisonneuve). 8vo. pp. xi. and 199.   **A.**
[Against Christianity as Semitic.]

Gerhard, C. J. Paul.

189. Lessing und Christus! Ein Friedenswort an Israel. Breslau, 1881 (Max). 8vo. pp. 31.   **C.**

Germanicus [pseudonym].

190. Die Frankfurter Juden und die Aussaugung des Volkswohlstandes. Eine Anklage wider die Agiotage und wider den Wucher. 4te Auflage. Leipzig, 1880 (Glaser und Garte). 8vo. pp. 95.   **A.**

191. Der neueste Raub am deutschen Nationalwohlstand. (Neuer Börsen schwindel, 2tes Heft.) Frankfurt-a-M. 1881. (H. B. xxi. 49.)   **A.**

192. Die Rothschildgruppe und der "Monumentale" Conversionschwindel von 1881. Eine zweite Anklage wider die Agiotage. Frankfurt-a-M. 1881 (E. Richter). 8vo. pp. 58.   **A.**

Gladius, Dr. [pseud. = Glück.]

192a. A tisza-eslári ugy ismerelten hullaja. Oroosi szakoélemény a közzetett bonczlelet alapján. Budapest, 1882 (K.) 8vo. pp. 38. **P.**
[The unknown corpse of Tisza Eszlar. Medical report founded on the dissections published.]

Glogau, Otto.

193. Des Reiches Noth und der neue Culturkampf. 3ᵗᵉ Auflage. Osnabrück, 1880. **A.**
[V. Periodicals. Berlin—Culturkämpfer. No. 379.]

Glück, Dr. J. (Landesrabbiner in Oldenburg).

194. Ein Wort an den Herrn Prof. H. von Treitschke. Oldenburg, 1880 (Schmidt). 8vo. pp. 16. **P.**

Goldenberg, Berisch.

194a. Die Assimilation der Juden. Tarnopol, 1883. 8vo. pp. 12. **P.**

Goldenstein, O.

195. Brody und die russisch-jüdische Emigration. Nach eigener Beobachtung. Frankfurt-a-M. 1882 (Kauffmann). 8vo. pp. 30. **P.**

Goldman, Julius.

196. Report on the Colonization of Russian Refugees in the West. (To the Hebrew Emigrants' Aid Society of the United States.) New York, 1882 (Evening Post Printing Office). 8vo. pp. 35. **P.**

Goldschmidt, Dr. J. (Rabbiner in Weilburg).

197. Ueber die Zukunft und Berechtigung des Judenthums, 1883 (1882). Leipzig (Heuser). 8vo. pp. 41. **P.**

Gonne, Louis.

198. L'Agitation Antisémitique en Allemagne. In *Revue générale de Belgique.* March 1, 1881. **P.**

Graetz, Prof. Dr. H.

199. Shylock in der Sage, im Drama und in der Geschichte. Krotoschin, 1880. 8vo. pp. 40. **P.**

Graetz, Prof. Dr. H.—*continued.*

200. Offener Brief an Herrn Prof. H. v. Treitschke. In
Schlesische Zeitung. Dec. 1879. **P.**

Grant, Charles.

201. The Jewish Question in Germany. In *Contemporary
Review.* March, 1881. pp. 366-384. **P.**

Grau, Prof. Dr. R. F.

202. Die Judenfrage und ihr Geheimniss. Gütersloh,
1881 (Bertelsmann). 8vo. pp. 56. **A.**

Gronsilliers, H. de.

203. Gegen Virchow und Genossen oder Offenbarung
und Wissen, 1880 (Polenz). 8vo. pp. 38. **A.**
[Founded on Spiritualism.]

204. Nathan der Weise und die Anti-Semiten Liga.
Berlin, 1880 (Polenz). 8vo. pp. 32. **A.**

Gruber, B. (Pastor in Reichenbach).

205. Christ und Israelit. Ein Friedenswort zur Judenfrage.
5te unveränderte Auflage mit vorgedrucktem Hand-
schreiben Sr. Kais. Kgl. Hoheit des Kronprinzen.
Reichenbach, 1880 (Hage und Gunzel). 8vo. pp. 23. **P.**

206. Der neue Sturm der Judenfrage. Reichenbach,
1880. 8vo. pp. 23. (H. B. xxi. 49). **P.**
[? 1st edition of preceding Number.]

Grumbkow, R. v.

207. Die Judenfrage vor Gericht. Klage des deutsch-
israelitischen Gemeindebunds in Leipzig gegen Autor
und Verleger der "Egon Waldegg'schen Judenfrage."
Nach den Processacten veröffentlicht. Dresden, Grumbkow, 1883. 8vo. pp. 33. **A.**

Grünebaum, Dr. E. (Rabbiner zu Landau).

208. Die Sittenlehre des Judenthums andern
Bekenntnissen gegenüber. Nebst dem geschichtlichen
Nachweise über Entstehung und Bedeutung des
Pharaismus und dessen Verhältniss zum Stifter der
christlichen Religion. 2te sehr vermehrte Auflage.
Strassburg, 1878 (Schneider). 8vo. pp. xxxvi. and 448.
P.

Güdemann, M.

209. Kinderschlächter. In *Wiener Allg. Zeitung*, 5 and
9 July, 1882. (H. B. xxi. 125.) **P.**

Gutsmuths, Freimund (Herausgegeber).

210. Wissenschaftliche Beiträge zur Judenfrage. Patriotische Untersuchungen. I. Die Juden vom Standpunkte
der christlichen Sittlichkeit betrachtet von A. Frantz.
II. Zwischenbemerkungen zur Judenfrage von Constantin Frantz. Berlin, n.d. (A. Klein.) 8vo. pp. 192.
A.

Hamburger, Dr. J.

211. Zurückweisung der Blutbeschuldigung. In *Realen-
cyclopädie für Bibel und Talmud*. II. pp. 1315–21. **P.**

Hammer, Dr. A. Th.

212. Juda und die deutsche Gesellschaft. Eines freisinnigen
Mannes Gedanken über die Judenfrage. Berlin, 1881
8vo. pp. 46. **A.**

Hapke, Prediger.

213. Die wahre Toleranz. Vortrag. (Staatssocialist,
1880.) 4to. pp. 3. (H. B. xx. 77.) **A.**

Hartmann, E. von.

214. Das religiöse Bewusstsein der Menschheit im
Stufengang seiner Entwicklung. Berlin, 1882 (Duncker).
8vo. pp. 627. (*Das norddeutsche Judenthum*, pp.
531–539, especially *Die Irreligiosität des Reformjuden-
thums*, p. 538.) **A.**

Hauff, Wilhelm.

215. Jud-Süss. Novelle. Berlin, 1881 (Ruppel). 12mo.
pp. 72. (Reprint.) **A.**

Heffel, Ehrenfried.

216. Der Verfall unserer wirthschaftlichen Zustände.
Gesammelte Vorträge und Aufsätze über handels-
politische, gewerbliche und sociale Fragen. Berlin, 1877
(M. A. Niendorf). 8vo. pp. 2 and 84. **A.**

Hegyesy, Eyula.

216a. A zsido hittan es talmud hatasa a tarsadalomra.
Debreczin (K.) 12mo. pp. 16. **A.**

[The influence of Judaism and the Talmud on society.]

Hellenbach, L. B.

217. Die Anti-semitische Bewegung. Leipzig, 1883
(1882) Besser. 8vo. pp. 55. (Einleitung, p. 3. 1. Der
jüdische Glaube. 2. Das jüdische Capital, 12. 3. Die
jüdische Presse, 19. 4. Die Solidarität der Juden, p.
36.) **A.**

Heman, Dr. C. F.

218. Die historische Weltstellung der Juden und die
moderne Judenfrage. Abdruck aus der conservativen
Monatsschrift, 1881. Mai und Juni, Leipzig, 1881
(Hinrichs). 8vo. pp. 76. **A.**

219. Die religiöse Weltstellung des jüdischen Volkes.
Leipzig, 1882 (Hinrichs). 8vo. pp. x. and 130. **A.**

Henrici, Dr. Ernst.

220. Toleranz und nationale Ehre. Rede gehalten am
10 Feb. 1881. Berlin, 1881 (Schulze). 8vo. pp. 13. **A.**

221. Was ist der Kern der Judenfrage? Vortrag
gehalten am 13 Januar, 1880. Berlin, 1881. (Verlag
der "Wahrheit.") 8vo. pp. 14. **A.**

222. Wie hat sich die Bevölkerung Berlins bei den
bevorstellenden Reichstagswahlen zu verhalten? Zugleich
ein Mahnwort an alle deutschen Wähler. Rede gehalten
am 17 Feb. 1881, zu Berlin. Berlin, 1881 (Schulze).
8vo. pp. 14. **A.**

Herman, Otto (Member of Hungarian Parliament).

223. Judenverfolgung und Psychiatrie. Budapest, 1881.
(Grill). 8vo. pp. 26. **A.**

[From Hungarian journal "Egyetértés."]

34

34

Herzfeld, M.

224. Die Emancipation der Juden in Rümanien, oder 888 von 300,000. Vienna, 1880. 8vo. pp. 16. [H. B. xx. 77.] **P.**

Herzfield, M.

224a. Das Skeker Bilbul Esztér und Haman: interessante Hirtenbriefe. Wien, 1883 (Herzfeld). 8vo. pp. 15. **P.**
[Relating to the affair of Tisza-Eszlar.]

Heuch, Rev. Prof. F. C. (of Christiania).

225. Reform-jüdische Polemik gegen das Christenthum im Gewande moderner Aesthetik. Flensburg, 1880. [H. B. xxi. 55.] **A.**
[? Translated from Norwegian or Danish.]

Heyse, W. L.

226. Ansichten der Juden. 2te Auflage. Berlin, 1877. **A.**

Hildesheimer, J.

227. Die jüdische Solidarität. Vortrag gehalten im Séfath-Emeth-Verein. Berlin, 1880. 8vo. pp. 35. [H. B. xx. 30.] **P.**

Hillebrand, Karl.

228. Halbbildung und Gymnasialreform. In *Deutsche Rundschau.* Bnd. 18. Berlin, 1879. **P.**
[Translated into English, *Contemporary Review*, 1880.]

Hoffmann, Moritz.

228a. A Semiták es Antisemiták. Felvilagositásul es megszivlelésül. Budapesth, 1883 (K.) 8vo. pp. 80. **P.**
[Semites and Antisemites. An exposition and encouragement.]

Hoffmnan, Prof. Dr. Paul [Rechtslehrer der Budapester Universität.]

228b. A zsidó Kérdés megbeszelva. . . . . Budapest, 1882 (K). 8vo. pp. 51. **P.**
[The Jewish Question discussed. . .]

Holländer, J.

229. Das Judengemetzel in Bulgarien. Rede am 8 Tage des Laubhüttenfestes. Posen, 1877. 8vo. pp. 17. **P.**

Holthof, Dr. Ludwig.

230. Der russische Vulkan. Ein Versuch zur Erklärung der Zustände und Geistesströmungen im modernen Russland. Frankfurt-a-M. 1882 (Morgenstern). 8vo. pp. 79. **P.**

["VIII. Die Unterdrückungen in Polen und die Judenhetze."]

Hommel, Fritz.

231. Die Semiten und ihre Bedeutung für die Kultur-geschichte. Mit drei Farbenkärtchen. Leipzig, 1881 (Schultze). 8vo. pp. viii. and 68, and 4 Maps. **P.**

[Touches on Jewish Question, pp. viii. and 67-8.]

Hugo, Victor.

232. Appeal to French Nation May 31st, 1882, signed by V. H. as President of the *Comité de secours pour les Israélites de Russie*. **P.**

233. Letter in Parisian papers of 17th June, 1882. **P.**

234. *Torquemada, Drame.* Paris, 1882. **P.**

[Containing scene in which Jews of Spain protest against tyranny.]

Hutten, Ulrich [pseud.]

234a. Das Judenthum in Oesterreich Ungarn. Eine nationalhistorische Studie. Budapest, 1882 (Bartalits). 8vo. pp. 138 (K). **A.**

Hyndman, H. M.

235. The Dawn of a Revolutionary Epoch. In *Nine-teenth Century*, January, 1881. **? A.**

[Devotes couple of pages to the Jews. "Not the slightest influence on the side of revolution will be that of the Jew."]

Israel, Rabbi Menasseh ben.

236. Gegen die Verleumder! Eine Stimme aus dem 17 Jahrhundert. Rabbi Menasseh ben Israel's "Rettung der Juden." 1 Theil, übersetzt von Moses Mendelssohn. Bamberg, 1882 (Hepple). 8vo. pp. 32. **P.**

Illustrations.

237. Humoristisch-satirisches Bilderbuch für die Anti-liberalen Wähler. Berlin, 1881 (M. Schulze). Oblong 8vo. p. 24. **A.**

[With 19 Cartoons from *Skizzenbuch der "Warheit,"* No. 240.]

238. Facetiæ Latinæ. De institutione studentica. De osculis. Berlin, 1881. (Verlag der "*Warheit.*") 8vo. pp. 28. **A.**

[At back "Bilder vom deutschen Parnass. No. 1. (= Carica-ture of Paul Lindau.) Ein Deutscher Parnassauer."]

239. Illustrirte Flugblätter, Nos. 1, 2, 3 aus der "*Wahr-heit.*" **A.**

240. *Skizzenbuch der "Wahrheit."* Jahrgang, 1880. 4te Auflage. Oblong 8vo. pp. 30, with 28 Antisemitic sketches. **A.**

240a. ———— ——— ———— Jahrgang, 1882.

Istoczy, G.

240b. 12 röpirat. Havi folyoirat. 1 fuzet. Budapest, 1880 (Bartalits). 8vo. pp. 48. **A.**

[V. Also Nos. 44 (Manifest) and 490 (Statutes).]

Janasz, Adolf.

241. Die Zukunft des Volkes Israel. Berlin, 1882. (Bonillon.) 8vo. pp. 15. **C.**

Jellinek, Dr. A.

242. Franzosen über Juden. Zweite Auflage. Wien, 1880 (Löwy). 8vo. pp. xxvi. and 36. **P.**

[First edition went out of print in five days.]

243. Der Talmudjude. Reden. I. Womit beginnt und womit schliesst der Talmud. 8vo. pp. 14. II. Die Lebensfülle des Talmuds. 8vo. pp. 14. Wien (D. Löwy) 1882. **P.**

[III. & IV. have also appeared. Has been translated into Hungarian.]

244. Organisation gegen Organisation. Wien, 1882 (Löwy). **P.**

Joel, Dr. M.

245. Offener Brief an Herrn Prof. Heinrich v. Treitschke 7ᵗᵉ Auflage. Breslau, 1879. 8vo. pp. 16. **P.**

Jolenberg, L.

246. Ein zeitgemässes Wort an unsere christlichen Mit-bürger, die gesammte "Judenfrage" betreffend. Berlin, 1881 (Selbstverlag). 12mo. pp. 24. **P.**

[Cf. Anon. No. 18, Briefwechsel.]

Judäus [pseudonym].

247. Was müssen wir Juden thun? Zürich, 1881 (Trüb.). 12mo. pp. 57. **P.**

Jungfer, Hans.

248. Die Juden unter Friedrich dem Grossen. Nach urkundlichen Quellen. Leipzig, 1880. 8vo. pp. 47. (H. B. xx. 78.) **A.**

Junius [pseudonym].

249. Das Judenthum und die Tagespresse. Ein Mahnwort in ernster Stunde. Leipzig, 1879 (Junge). 8vo. pp. 32. **A.**

250. Paul Lindau und das literarische Judenthum. Ein Controvers-predigt aus der Gegenwart. Leipzig, 1879. (H.B. xix. 75). **A.**

Jurisconsultus [pseudonym].

251. The Crisis in Jewish History. 8vo. pp. 12. **P.**

[Three articles reprinted from *Jewish Chronicle*, 16 and 30 December, 1881, and 13 January, 1882.]

Justus, Dr. [pseudonym.]

251a. Judenspiegel, oder 100 neuenthüllte, heutzutage noch geltende den Verkehr der Juden mit den Christen betreffende Gesetze der Juden ; mit einer die Entstehung und Weiter-entwickelung der jüdischen Gesetze darstel-lenden, höchst interessanten Einleitung. Dritte Auflage. Paderborn, 1883 (Bonifacius Druckerei). 16mo. **A.**

Kalthoff, Dr.

252. Judenthum, Christenthum. Rede. Berlin, 1879.
8vo. pp. 18. (H. B. xxi. 50.) **P.**

253. Die neueste Massregel zur Bekämpfung des Judenthums. Vortrag gehalten im Saale des Handwerker-
Vereins zu Berliu. Berlin, 1880 (Würzburg). 8vo.
pp. 20. **P.**

Kaszonyi, Dániel.

253a. Solymozi Eszter a tisza-eszlari véráldozat Tarza-
dalmeregeny a jelenkorbol [Esther Solymosi, the Blood
Sacrifice of Tisza Eszlar. A social romance of the present day]. Budapest, 1882 (G. Petrik). 8vo. pp. 225
(K.) **A.**

[Also translated into German *sub-titulo*; *Esther Solymosi, das
Blutopfer von Tisza Eszlár. Socialroman aus der Gegenwart.*
Budapest, 1882. Petrik pp. vi. and 257 (K.)].

Katz, Manus [=K. Amitti, q.v.]

254. Offener Brief an den Recensenten - Anonymus
"Schewet" Herrn Landrabbiner Dr. Kroner in Stadt-
lengsfeld. Berlin, 1882 (Issleib.) **A.**

[In reference to a criticism in *Jüd. Litteraturblatt*, No. 2, 1882.
Cf. No. 9.]

[Kauffmann, Prof. Dr. D.]

255. Ein Wort in Vertrauen an Hrn. Hofprediger Stöcker
von Einem dessen Name Nichts zur Sache thut. Berlin,
1880. 8vo. pp. 20. [H. B. xx. 31.] **P.**

255a. Die Lichter am Abend. Predigt. 1880. 8vo.
pp. 15. **P.**

255b. Vom jüdischen Katechismus. Budapest, 1884
(Zilahy). 8vo. pp. 19. **P.**

Kauffman, Jaques.

256. Deux propositions modestes et opportunes et appel
aux Roumains de tous les rites. Jassy, 1879 (Goldner).
8vo. pp. 19. [H. B. xx. 85.] **P.**

Kayserling, Dr. M.

257. Die Blutbeschuldigung von Tisza Eszlar. Buda-Pesth, 1882. 8vo. pp. 16. **P.**

258. Der Wucher und das Judenthum. Buda-Pesth, 1883 (Wodianer). 8vo. pp. 20. **P.**

Kelchner, E.

259. Wozu der Lärm? Ein Beitrag zur Klärung der sogenannten Judenfrage. Frankfurt/a/M., 1881. 8vo. pp. 24. [H. B. xxi. 50.] **P.**

Kellog, Rev. Prof. S. H.

259a. The Jews, Prediction and Fulfilment, an Argument for the Times. London, 1883 (Nisbet). pp. xx. and 289. **C.**

[An article by the same appeared in the *New Englander*, May, 1881, with the title 'The Jewish Question in Europe,' republished in the *British and Foreign Evangelical Review*, October, 1881.]

Klein, Dr. Gottleib (Rabbiner in Elbing).

260. Zur "Judenfrage." Unsere Anforderungen an das Christenthum des Herrn Stöcker. Zurich, 1880 (Schabelitz). 8vo. pp. 23. **P.**

Kleist, Dr. L.

261. Der Apostel Stöcker, seine Jünger und der deutsche Bürgerkrieg. Ein Beitrag zur Entwickelungsgeschichte der Antisemitischen Bewegung. Berlin, 1881 (Stuhr). 8vo. pp. 26. **P.**

Köhler, Paul.

262. Die Verjudung Deutschlands und der Weg zur Rettung. Noch einmal ein Wort für und wider. "W. Marr: der Sieg des Judenthums über das Germanenthum." Stettin, 1880 (Brandner). 8vo. pp. 62. **A.**

Kohler, Dr. K.

263. Deutschland und die Juden. Der Jüdische Kosmopolitanismus. New York, 1881 (Steiger). 8vo. pp. 15. **?A.**

Kohn, Samuel.

263a. Mit tegyünk az ellenünk intezet támadá-sokkal szemben? [What are we to do in face of the attacks directed against us?] Budapesth, 1880 (Zilahy). 8vo. pp. 10. [Sermon. H. B. xx. 78.] **P.**

Kolkmann, Dr. Joseph.

264. Die gesellschaftliche Stellung der Juden. Dritte Auflage mit einem Vorwort. Zum Gedächtniss Joseph Kolkmann's. Berlin, 1881 (Schilke). 8vo. pp. 64. **P.**

Kopelowitz, Jacob.

264a. Bibel und Talmud oder: Ist der rituelle Mord möglich? Wien, 1883 (Schlossberg). 8vo. pp. 40. **P.**

Kühn [pseudonym].

265. Zu Schutz und Trutz. Zeitgedichte. 4te Auflage. Berlin, 1881 (O. Lorentz). 16mo. pp. i. and 36. **A.**

[Jüd. Wahlspruch, p. 13, Des Juden Vaterland, p. 18, Den Philosemiten, p. 21, Zaukönige, pp. 31-36 (G. v. Amyntor—P. Lindau —O. Blumenthal—J. Rodenberg—B. Auerbach—G. Ebers—Fanny Lewald—P. Cassel—J. Offenbach).]

Kurrein, Adolf.

266. *Maggid Leadam.* Die Menschenlehre des Judenthums. Der Mensch, die Menschlichkeit und die Menschheit. Zehn Reden. Wien, 1882 (Schlossberg). 8vo. pp. 201. **P.**

Laister, James.

267. Why Jews are Persecuted. In *Modern Thought*, May and June, 1882. **A.**

267a. The Imperishable Jew. In *Modern Thought*, Dec. 1883. **A.**

Laat, van der.

268. In *Révue Catholique de Louvain*, 15 March, 1880. **P.**

Landsberger, Dr. Julius (Prediger zu Berlin).

269. Wahrheit, Recht und Liebe. Eine Kanzelrede für
Freunde und Feinde des Judenthums. Berlin, 1881
(Peiser). 8vo. pp. 16. **P.**

Lázár, Prof. Dr. Julius.

270. Das Judenthum in seiner Vergangenheit und
Gegenwart. Mit besonderem Hinblick nach Ungarn.
Zweite Auflage. Berlin, 1880 (Hentze). 8vo. pp. ii.
and 127. **A.**

Lazarus, Emma.

271. Russian Christianity *v.* Modern Judaism. In *The
Century Magazine*, May, 1882, pp. 48–56. **P**
[Answering article by Mad. Ragozin No. 404.]

272. The Jewish Question. In *Century Magazine*, Feb.
1883. **P.**

272a. Songs of a Semite. New York, 1882 (Office
" American Hebrew "). 8vo. pp. 80. **P.**
[" The crowing of the red cock," p. 52, and " In Exile," p. 53,
refer to Russian persecutions.]

Lazarus, Prof. Dr. M.

273. Unser Standpunkt. Zwei Reden an seine Religions-
genossen am 1 und 16 Dez. 1880 gehalten. Berlin,
1881 (Stuhr). 8vo. pp. 40. **P.**

274. Was heisst National ? Ein Vortrag. Zweite
Auflage. Berlin, 1880 (Dümmler). 8vo. pp. 58 and 3.
[In answer to Treitschke, No. 506.] **P.**

Lehmann, Emil.

274a. Ueber die judenfeindliche Bewegung in Deutsch-
lande. Dresden, 1880. **P.**
[See also George Eliot, No. 168.]

Lehnhardt, Erich.

274b. Die antisemitische Bewegung in Deutschland,
besonders in Berlin, nach Voraussetzungen, Wesen,
Berechtigung und Folgen dargelegt. Zürich, 1884
(Verlagsmagazin). 8vo. pp. 102. **A.C.**

Leib, Mausche Mochuls (zu Richmond in Süd-
afrika. ? pseud.)

275. Ein Wort an die deutschen Juden. Zurich, 1881
(Schmidt). 8vo. pp. 18.   **P.**

Lerique, J.

276. Das Judenthum in der deutschen Literatur.
[Frankfurter zeitgemässige Broschüren. Bnd. III. Hft.
9.] Frankfurt/a/M., 1882 (Fresser). 8vo. pp. 34. **A.**

Leroy-Beaulieu.

277. Les troubles antisémitiques ; la persecution des
juifs en Russie. In *Revue politique et literaire.* Paris,
1880, No. 20, p. 609.   **P.**

Leschmann, G. F.

278. Hofprediger Stöcker oder : Meine persönlichen
Erlebnisse unter den Christlich-socialen in Berlin. Offen-
bach/a/M., 1881. [H. B. xxi. 127.]   **P.**

Letson, Dr. E.

279. Anti-Stöcker. Offner Brief und Nachwort. Zweite
Auflage. Berlin, 1879 (Schildberger). 8vo. pp. 16. **P.**

Levi, Giulio, G. [Avvocato.]

279a. La questione semitica e la sua possibile soluzione
Lettera d' un semita al sig. G. B. Borelli. Turin,
1883 (Botta).   **P.**

Lewin, Dr. A., Rabbiner.

280. Naturwissenschaft oder Judenhass. Breslau, 1880
(Leuckart). 8vo. pp. 29.   **P.**

Lichtenstein-Anageton, Edmund.

281. Zur Abwehr. Das antisemitische "Deutsche Tage-
Blatt" im Lichte der Wahrheit. Schönebeck, 1882
(Wolff).   **P.**

Lindauer, Saul [pseud. of Dr. Willy Böhm].

282. Die Schöpfungsgeschichte der "Gräfin Lea." Ein
deutscher Festnachtsschwank. Berlin, 1881 (O. Lorentz).
8vo. pp. 36.   **A.**
[In verse.]

Linden, Gustav, von.

283. Der Sieg des Judenthums über das Germanenthum. Eine Widerlegung der W. Marr'schen Polemik in historischer und allgemeiner Beziehung, zugleich eine Mahnung an das deutsche Volk und an die deutschen Fürsten. 2 Auflage. Leipzig, 1879 (Körner). 8vo. pp. vi. and 41. **A.**

Ljutostanski, J. J.

283a. The question as to the use of Christian blood for ritual purposes by Jewish sects in connection with the general relations of Judaism and Christianity [Russian]. Moscow, 1876. 8vo. pp. x. and 285. [H. B. xviii. 126.] **A.**

Lippert, Julius.

283b. Der Antisemitismus. Prag, 1883. **? P.**

["Sammlung gemeinnütziger Vortraege. Herausgegeben vom deutschen Verein zur Verbreitung gemeinnütziger Kenntnisse. No. 88."]

Loeb, Isidore [Secrétaire de l'Alliance israélite universelle, Paris].

284. La situation des Israélites en Turquie, en Serbie et en Roumanie. Paris, 1877 (Baer). 8vo. pp. v. and 471.

[An admirable compilation, containing everything of importance up to date. May be considered second edition of *La situation des israélites en Servie et en Roumanie*, Paris, 1876 (Chaix), 8vo. pp. 141.]

Löwenfeld, Dr. S.

285. Die Wahrheit über der Juden Antheil am Verbrechen. Auf grund amtlicher Statistik. Berlin, 1881 (Stuhr). 8vo. pp. 16. **P.**

[An answer to Anon. No. 31, *Der Juden Antheil am Verbrechen.*]

Löwy, Josef.

286. Wucher und Wucherer. Gross Kanizsa. 1880 (Selbstverlag). **P.**

Ludolf [pseudonym].

287. Wie Berolinensis Silesiacus der Dichter der
"jüdischen Referendar" ward. Löbau, 1879. 8vo. pp.
12. [H. B. xx. 31.]   **A.**

M. Gy.

287a. Solymosi Eszter vagy a Tisza-Eszlári giulkosság.
(E. S. or the Murder at Tisza Eszlar.) Budapesth,
1882. 8vo. pp. 32 (K.)   **P.**

M., J. H.

288. Juden, Studenten, Professoren. Frage und Ant-
wortspiel. Leipzig, 1881 (C. W. Vollrath). 8vo. pp.
52.   **P.**

[Against *Die studentische Petition*, No. 64.]

Maass, M.

289. Die Mischehe. Die einzig wirksamen Mittel einer
dauernden Vereinigung zwischen der jüdischen und
christlichen Bevölkerung Deutschlands. Löbau, 1880.
[H. B. xx. 78.]   **A.**

Macaulay, Thomas Babington, Lord.

290. The Civil Disabilities of the Jews herausgegeben
von Dr. F. Fischer. Berlin, 1880 (Simion).   **P.**

[Intended as an English reading book, and at the same time as
a contribution to the Jewish Question.]

Macdonald, James [formerly at Shanghai,China.]

291. Jewish Cruelty in London. Coroner's Justice ! ! !
In re John Humphreys, chief Coroner for Middlesex, etc.,
etc., and the killing of little Alice Moss. 8vo. pp. 28,
with rough engraving on title-page, privately printed. **A.**

[Takes up case of the father of a little girl accidentally run over
by a Jewish cabman. Pp. 21-24, an account of a ship saved off
Corea! Postscript, July 13th, 1882. "In consequence of the continued persecution of Jews on the Continent, the publication of
this case has been postponed."]

Maier, Gustav.

292. Mehr Licht. Ein Wort zur Judenfrage an unsere Christlichen Mitbrüger. Ulm, 1881 (H. Kerler) 8vo. pp. 25. **P.**

Mandl, L.

293. Psychologie zum Verständniss der Antisemitismus Treue Worte an Freund und Feind. Wein, 1882 (Selbstverlag). **P.**

Marbach, Prof. Oswald.

294. Ueber die sittlichen Ausartungen und Bedrohungen des Culturlebens in der Gegenwart. (Separatausdruck aus der freimaurischen Monatschrift "Am Reisbreite,") Leipzig. 1880 (Zechel). [H.B. xx. 78.] **?P.**

Marczali, Mihály.

294a. Fegy vereink rosozakarörukellen. Ujévi beszed Budapest, 1882 (Aigner). 8vo. pp. 11. K. **P.**

[Our weapons against evil-wishers. New Year's sermon.]

Marczianyi, Georg von.

295. Esther Solymosi oder der jüdisch-rituelle Jungfermord in Tissa Esslar. Autorisirte deutsche Uebersetzung aus dem Ungarischen. Nebst einer Abbildung der Synagoge in Tissa Esslar. Berlin, 1882 (M. Schulze) 12mo. pp. 52. **A.**

Marr II. [pseudon.]

296. Teitteles Teutonicus. Harfenklänge aus dem vermauschelten Deutschland. Mit 20 künstlerischen Illustrationen und 1 Titelbild. Zweite Auflage. Bern, 1879 (Costenoble). **A.**

Marr, W. [See *Periodicals. Germany, Deutsche Wacht.* Marr wrote a *Judenspiegel* as early as 1862.]

297. Der Judenkrieg, seine Fehler und wie er zu organisiren ist. Zweiter Theil von "Der Sieg des Judenthums u.s.w." Chemnitz, 1880 (Schweitzner). 8vo. pp. 32.

[Also as *Antisemitische Hefte*, No. 1.] **A.**

Marr, W.—*continued.*

298. Vom jüdischen Kriegschauplatz. Eine Streitschrift·
Vierte Auflage. Bern, 1879 (Costenoble). 8vo. pp. 48·
[Against Perinhardt, No. 367.]   **A.**

299. Juden und Socialdemokraten. Chemnitz, 1881
(Schweitzner). 8vo. pp. 32.   **A.**
[Also as *Antisemitische Hefte, No. 2, Goldene Ratten und rothe
Mäule.*]

300. Oeffnet die Augen Ihr deutschen Zeitungsleser.
Ein unentbehrliches Büchlein für jeden deutschen Zeit.
ungsleser. Chemnitz, 1880 (Schweitzner). 8vo. pp. 32.
[Also as *Antisemitische Hefte,* No. 3.]   **A.**

301. Der Sieg des Judenthums über das Germanenthum.
Vom nicht confessionellen Standpunkt aus betrachtet.
Zwölfte Auflage vermehrt durch ein Vorwort des
Verfassers an Israel. Bern, 1879 (Costenoble). 8vo. **A.**

302. Der Weg zum Siege des Germanenthums über das
Judenthum (Vierte Auflage von " Wählet keinen Juden ").
Berlin, 1880 (O. Hentze). 8vo. pp. 48.   **A.**
[A fifth edition appeared in 1881 as "Agitations-ausgabe"
for 30 pf.]

Matók, B.

302a. A Zsidokérdés. Nro 2. Tortėnelmi tàrsadalmi ės
törvemyer szempontból tárgyalva. Budapesth, 1881.
8vo. pp. 135 (K).   **A.**
[The Jewish Question, No. 2. Treated from an historical, social,
and legal point of view.]

Maurer, A.

303. Das Börsen-Raubritterthum in Verbindung mit
dem Antisemitenthum unserer Zeit. Die Mittel für ihre
Besiegung. Eine wohlgemeinte und rechtzeitige Mahnung
an das deutsche Judenthum. Wernheim (Baden), 1882
(Ackermann). 8vo. pp. 17.   **A.**
["Stellenweise ganz neu, im uebrigen . . . . ein Auszug aus . . . .
Das Tabakmonopol und Parasitenthum der Tabaksindustrie.
2 Auflagen, April und Mai, 1882."]

Mazaroz, J. P.

304. La genése moderne ou religion économique et syndicale de Moïse. Paris, 1877. 8vo. pp. 192.   A.

Medals.

305. (*a*) Brass. *Obverse*—Pilgrim hat and staff, with motto, "Der echte Deutsche Mann mag keinen Juden leiden, Berlin, 1881." *Reverse*—Jew "taking a sight." Motto, "Doch sein Vermögen hätt' er gern."
(*b*) Brass. *Obverse*—Arms of Berlin.   "Berlin, 1880-81.   Hep! Hep!" *Reverse*—"Hoch Stöcker, Förster, Henrici. Vivant sequentes."
(*c*) Nickel. *Obverse*—"Die Chuzbe ist des Jüden Schmuck." *Reverse*—"Muth zeiget auch der Mameluk. Berlin, 1881."
(*d*) *Obverse*—"Vienna urbs a Turcis liberata, MDCLXXXIII." *Reverse* — "A Judæis capta, MDCCCLXXXIII."   A.

Meuthner, Fritz.

306. Der neue Ahasverus. Roman. 2 Bände. 1882. P.

Meyer, Dr. Rudolph.

307. Politische Gründer und die Corruption in Deutschland. Leipzig, 1877 (Bidder). 8vo. pp. 204.   A.

Meyer, Dr. S.

308. Ein Wort an Herrn Professor Heinrich von Treitschke. Berlin, 1880 (Stuhr).   P.

308a. Völkerrecht und Humanität und die orientalische Frage der Israeliten im Orient. Berlin, 1877.   P.

309. Zurückweisung des dritten judenfeindlichen Artikels des Herrn Professor Heinrich von Treitschke. Berlin, 1880 (Stuhr).   P.

Molchow, C.

310. Jesus ein Reformer des Judenthums. Zürich, 1880.   C.

Mommsen, Th. [Prof. Dr.]

311. Auch ein Wort über unser Judenthum. Berlin, 1880 (Weidmann). 8vo. pp. 18.   P.

Montefiore, Claude.

312.   Is Judaism a Tribal Religion ?   P.
In *Contemporary Review*, Oct. 1882. [Cf. Cobbe, No. 138.]

Morais, Miss Nina.

313.   Jewish Ostracism in America.   P.
In *North American Review* for September, 1881.

Morel, MM. [Brothers].

313a.   Les juifs de la Hongrie devant l'Europe.   Affaire
de Tisza-Eszlar.   Paris, 1883.   8vo. pp. 63.   P.

Moreniss, L.

314.   Die Colonisation der Juden in Russland und
Rumänien.   1881, Wien.   P.

Moses, Adolf.

315.   Prof. Dr. Hermann Cohen in Marburg.   Milwaukee
[U.S.], 1880.   8vo. pp. 13.   [H. B. xxi. 51.]   P.

Müller, Dr. Fr.

316.   Stöcker's angeblich ethisch-sociale Judenfrage.   Eine
allseitige Beleuchtung derselben vom politischen und
sittlichen Standpunkte aus mit besonderer Berücksichtig-
ung der Mischehe.   Zweite verbesserte Auflage.   Wurz-
burg, Dec. 1880.   8vo. pp. 77.   P.

Münz, Dr. L. (Rabbiner zu Kempen).

317.   Die modernen Anklagen gegen das Judenthum.
1880.   P.

Music.

318.   Berliner Couplets.   Verlag Oscar Linderer.   A.
Das genügt, Couplet von Oscar Linderer [6th Stanza.]
Die polnische Juden-Hochzeit.
Der boomwollne Hanschen, neue Parodie in jüdischer
    Mundart.
Jacob Leyser, unter'n Pantoffel.
Napolium Cohnheim's nächtliche Parade.
Der schone Wolfsohn als Don Juan.   Komischer
    SoloVortrag in Jüd.Mundart miturkomischem
    Couplet.

Music—*continued.*

319. Berliner Leier Kasten. Verlag, W. Horn. **A.**
   13. Die jüdischen Rekruten.
   24. Ich bin der Isaak Silberstein.
   25. Kümmt 'raus der Jüd.
   51. Jüdisches Ständschen.
   59. Ohn'ä ·Probe gaiht es nischt.
   60. ä Schmu'l macht sich grauss.
   68. Die jüdische Menagerie.

Nadyr, Rabbiner M. A.

320. Offener Brief eines polnischen Juden an den
   Redacteur Herrn Heinrich v. Treitschke, K. . . 14
   Dezember, 1879, Loebau (Skrzeczek). 8vo. pp. 28. **P.**

Naudh, H. [pseud. = **H. Nordmann,** v. *Anon.*
   No. 38.]

321. Israel im Heere. Berlin, 1879 (O. Hentze). 8vo.
   pp. 19. **A.**
   (Separat-Abdruck aus der Deutschen Wacht, Organ der anti-
   jüdischen Vereinigung.)

322. Minister Maybach und der "Giftbaum." Dritte
   Auflage. Berlin, 1880 (Hentze). 8vo. pp. 33. **A.**

323. Professoren über Israel, von Treitschke und
   Bresslau. Berlin, 1880 (O. Hentze). 8vo. pp. 29. **A.**

Neofito [Ex-rabbinico monaco greco. Pseud.]

323a. Il sangue christiano nei rite ebraici della moderna
   Sinagoga : rivelazioni. Versione dal greco del Prof.
   N. F. S. Prato, 1883 (Giachetti). 8vo. pp. 100 and
   portr. **A.**
   Qy. whether any Greek original exists ?
   [Translated into Dutch : *Het Christenbloed bij de Joodsche
   ritueele gebruiken der moderne synagoge. Onthullingen van den
   ex-Rabbijn Neofitus Grieksch Kloosterling. Naar de Italiaansche
   overzetting . . . . door den schrijver van* "*Laster of Misdaad ?*"
   Leyden, 1883 (van Leewen) 4to. pp. 40.] Also in Roumanian.

Neubauer, Dr. Adolf. M.A., Oxon.

324. Offener Brief an Herrn Professor Heinrich v.
   Treitschke. **P.**
   In *Vossische Zeitung,* 26 Dec. 1879.

Neumann, Marie [evangel. Schulvorsteherin zu Hanau.]

325. Ein Wort an die Frauen über die Judenfrage. In *Deutsche Hausfrauen Zeitung*, 26 Oct. 1879. [H. A. xix. 103.]
B.

Neumann, Dr. S.

326. Die Fabel von der jüdischen Masseneinwanderung. Ein Kapitel aus der preussischen Statistik. Zweite Auflage. Berlin, 1880 (Simion). 8vo. pp. 46.
P.

[Third edition also contains the following No.]

327. Nachschrift zur Fabel von der jüdischen Massenein-wanderung enthaltend : I. Antwort an Herrn Adolf Wagner ; II. Herr Heinrich v. Treitschke und seine jüdische Masseneinwanderung ; III. Die Antwort des Königl. preussischen statistischen Bureaus. Berlin, 1881 (Simion).
P

Neuman, W. [Lewi.]

328. Der Friede unter den Kindern der Bibel. Prag, 1882 (Brandeis). 8vo. pp. 31.
P.

Neustadt, P.

329. Zur jüdischen Feindesliebe. Breslau, 1879. 8vo. pp. 16. [H. B. xx. 78.]
P.

[Sonderabsdruck aus dem zwölften Bericht der hebräischen Unterrichtsanstalt.]

Newspapers.—See *Periodicals.*

[Outside England, only specially Antisemitic organs are given except 334*a* and 342*a* ; Jewish Papers in Singer, 480.]

Newspapers—Austro-Hungary—Buda Pesth.

329a. Fuggetlenseg. [? Weekly] in progress.
A.

Newspapers—Austria—Steyer.

329b. Die Judenfrage. [1882, weekly ?]
A.

Newspapers—Austria—Trieste.

329c. La Stafetta. 1883. [Weekly]
A.

Newspapers—Austria—Vienna.

330. Oesterreichische Volksfreund. Einzige Antijüdische Oesterreichische Zeitschrift. [Weekly, 1882.] **A.**

Newspapers—England—London.

330a. Christian and Jew. **A.**

[Said to be a newspaper secretly printed in England to "counsel a crusade against the Jews." Question asked thereon by Mr. R. Power, in House of Commons, 20 Feb. 1882. Sir William Harcourt reported letter received from the author, who says, "The Jews have established cigar shops all over London, by which they have ruined the legitimate trade, and usurped the whole of the tailoring trade; but the chief head of his indictment is that they have entered into a combination to make Baron Henry de Worms Prime Minister of Great Britain." Hansard's Parliamentary Debates, 3rd ser. vol. cclxvi. pp. 1098-9.]

331. Punch ; or, the London Charivari.

The anti-semitic Movement, Jan. 29, 1881, with illustration by Du Maurier.

Russian Jews. Feb. 11, 1882, with cartoon, by J. Tenniel.

332. The *Times* [from Palmer's Index.]

1876.

Jews and Eastern Question, 14th Oct. p. 11, c. 3 ; 16th Oct. p. 8, c. 3 ; 17th Oct. p. 6, c. 2 ; 18th Oct. p. 11, c. 2.

Jews and Mr. Gladstone on their Rights, 3rd Nov. p. 4, c. 6.

1877.

Jews and Eastern Question, 2nd Jan. p. 6, c. 5.

1878.

Jews in Russia, 14th Feb. 4*e.*
Jews in Eastern Europe, 17th June, 12*f.*

1879.

Jewish Farmers in Russia, 20th Nov. 5*f.*

1880.

Jews in Russia, 16th March, 4*a* ; 9th Aug. 11*a.*
Jews in Germany (Leaders), 18 Nov. 9*d*, 22 Nov. 9*d.*
Germany, Anti-semitic Agitation in, 22 Dec. 5*f.*

Newspapers—England—London—*continued.*
The Times, 1880—continued.

German Jews, Agitation Against, 15 Nov. 6*a* ; 18 Nov.
8*a* ; 19 Nov. 5*d* ; 20 Nov. 5*c* ; 22 Nov. 5*b* ; 23 Nov.
5*b* ; 24 N. 5*b* ; 25 N. 5*d* ; 30 N. 5*d* ; 3 Dec. 5*c* ;
13 D. 5*c* ; 21 D. 5*d*.
Germany, Jew Chase in, 19 Nov. 5*b*.
German Jews, Note about, 19 Nov. 6*b*.
Germany. Proceedings in Chambers, 23 Nov. 6*b*.
German Jews, Students of Berlin and, 2 Dec. 5*f*.

1881.

Jews in Russia, 23 May, 11*e* ; 7 June, 4*c* ; 16 June, 5*b*.
Distress in South Russia, 26 May, 7*e*.
Jews in Russia, Deputation of the Anglo-Jewish As-
sociation to Government about, 15 May, 12*d*.
Jews in Russia, Fund in aid of, 9 June, 7*d* ; 16 June, 5*f*.
Russia, Anti-Jewish Agitation in, 17 May, 5*c* ; 19 May,
5*f* ; 20 May, 5*f*.
Russian Anti-Jewish Demonstrations, 21 April, 5*d* ; 2
May, 7*f* ; 23 June, 7*d*.
Russian Attack on Jews at Odessa, 20 May, 5*d*.
Russia and the Jews, 29 April, 5*c* ; 30 April, 7*d* ; 16
June, 5*b* ; 2 May, 5*d* ; 9 May, 8*c* ; 10 May, 5*e* ; 11
May, 7*f* ; 12 May, 5*d* ; 16 May, 8*b* ; 28 May, 7*d* ; 31
May, 5*b* ; 6 June, 5*d*.
Russian Jews of Odessa ordered to Surrender their
Arms, 16 May, 8*b*.
Russian Jew baitings, 12 May, 5*e*.
Jewish Deputation to the Emperor, 24 May, 7*c*.
Germany. Jews, Unseemly Violence in Connection with,
3 Jan. 5*e* ; 12 J. 5*e* ; 17 J. 7*e* ; 17 J. 8*a* ; 20 J. 5*f* ;
1 Feb. 5*c* ; 2 F. 5*b* ; 4 F. 5*c* and *d* ; 17 F. 5*a* ; 22
F. 5*c* ; 12 Mar. 5*c* ; 24 M. 5*e*.
Mr. Lewisohn's Expulsion (Leader), 21 Aug. 9*e* ; 22 Aug.
4*d* ; 1 Sept. 9*f*.
Russia. Anti-Jewish Disturbance, 30 July, 5*d*.
Russia, Jews in, 5 Aug. 5*d* ; 15 Aug. 11*c* ; 16 A. 5*d* ;
18 A. 3*d* ; 30 A. 9*a* ; 1 Sept. 5*d* ; 6 S. 4*b* ; 9 S.,
4*e* ; 22 S. 9*c* ; 23 S. 5*f*.
Russian Jews, Note on, 4 July, 7*f*.
Russian Jews leaving for America, 11 July, 5*e*.

Newspapers—England—London—*continued.*

The Times, 1881—continued.

Russia. Jewish Agriculturist's Fund, Baron Gunzburg's Donation to, 11 July, 5*e.*
Russian Jews Relief Fund, 25 July, 6*f.*
Jews in Odessa, 22 Nov. 8*c.*
Jews in Russia, 31 Dec. 11*f.*
Russia, Jews in, 8 Oct. 5*f*; 11 O. 5*c*; 28 O. 9*f*; 10 Nov. 8*a*; 10 Dec. 5*d.*
Russia. Local Commission, Circular appointing, 3 Oct. 6*a.*
Russia on the Jewish Question, 7 Nov. 6*a.*

1882.

1st Quarter : Jan.—March.

Jews in Russia, 3 J. 6*c*; 7 J. 10*c*; 11 J. 4*a*; 13 J. 4*b*; 16 J. 8*c*; 17 J. 8*c*; 18 J. 10*c*; 19 J. 12*f*; 20 J. 9*b*; 21 J. 5*c*; 23 J. 4*f*; 24 J. 8*a*; 26 J. 8*c*; 28 J. 7*a*; 31 J. 7*f*; 31 J. 8*b*; 24 M. 5*b.*
Jews in Russia. Chief Rabbi appeals to the Jews for Subscriptions, 8 Feb. 10*f*; 9 F. 10*c.*
Jews in Russia. Consuls' Report of Persecution of Jews in Russia, 16 F. 7*d.*
Jews in Russia. Immigrants from Russia and Poland shipped to New York, 22 F. 10*f.*
Jews in Russia. Meeting of Sympathy at National Club, 25 F. 9*e.*
Jews in Russia, Meeting at Mansion House to form a Fund for, 23 J. 8*a*; 2 F. 4*c*; 3 F. 6*d*; 7 F. 6*d*; 10 F. 10*b*; 13 F. 6*c*; 21 F. 10*e*; 23 F. 8*a*; 27 F. 6*c*; 1 M. 6*e*; 8 M. 12*e*; 25 M. 14*b.*
Jews in Russia. Memorial of the Jews in England to the Emperor of Russia on the Persecution of the Russians, 25 J. 7*d.*
Jews in Russia, Official Correspondence on the Treatment of, in Russia, 20 F. 7*a*; 2 M. 11*a*; 3 M. 4*d.*
Jews in Russia, Outrages upon, at Warsaw, 4 J. 5*f.*
Jews in Russia, Oxford University on the Persecution of, 18 F. 4*a*; 27 F. 6*c.*

Newspapers—England—London—*continued.*

The Times, 1882—continued.
Jews in Russia, Persecution of, Notes on, 31 J. 8*b*; 7 F. 6*d*.
Jews in Russia, Meetings about, 2 F. 3*e*; 3 F. 5*d*; 4 F. 6*e*; 6 F. 9*f*; 11 F. 10*e*; 15 F. 5*d*; 16 F. 10*f*.
Jews in Russia, Press on the Oppression of the, 33 J. 6*a*.
Jewish Persecution, 11 J. 9*c*; 18 J. 9*c*; 2 F. 7*b*; 4 March, 9*c*. (Leading Articles.)
Russia, Jews from, Emigrate to Palestine as Farmers, 9 March, 5*d*.
Russian Jews, Notes about, 31 J. 7*f*; 4 F. 6*e*; 15 F. 4*e*; 29 M. 7*f*.
Russia, Jewish Refugees from, 11 F. 10*e*.
Russia. Law Prohibiting Jews to be Chemists in St. Petersburg being carried out, 28 M. 5*c*.
Russia. Migration of Jews to England, 13 F. 6*c*.
Adler (H.) On Jews in Russia, 19 J. 12*a*.
Asher (Dr. A.) Note on the Persecution of the Jews in Russia, 4 Feb. 6*e*.
Green (A. L.) On the Jews in Russia, 31 J. 7*f*; 1 F. 7*f*.
Löwy, (A.) On the Outrages on the Jews at Warsaw, 4 J. 5*f*.
Novikoff (Madame de) On Jews in Russia, 15 F. 4*e*.
Simon (John). On the Persecution of the Jews in Russia, 17 Jan. 8*c*.
Jews, Emigration to America, 28 J. 7*a*.
Jews, Emigration of, to England from Russia, 13 F. 6*c*.

2nd Quarter : April—June.

Jews, Russian, in Brody, Terrible State of, 22 M. 8*a*; 29 M. 6*b*; 31 M. 5*f*; 31 M. 8*a*; 1 J. 6*a*; 2 J. 5*d*; 3 J. 7*f*; 6 J. 5*e*.
Jews, Russian, Emigration of, Notes on, 31 M. 8*b*; 26 J. 7*a*.
Jews, Russian, Persecution of, Meeting at the Mansion House to raise a Fund for their Relief, 7 M. 4*d*; 20 M. 4*a*; 7 J. 5*e*; 22 J. 7*f*; 24 J. 12*f*; 29 J. 11*e*.
Jews, Russian, Refugees, 8 J. 7*d*.
Jews, Russian, Appeal for Clothes, etc., 22 M. 9*d*.

Newspapers—England—London—*continued.*

The Times, 1882—continued.
Jews, Russian, Special Performance at the Gaiety to assist, 9 J. 9*f.*
Germany. Jews Emigration, 21 A. 5*a.*
America. Hebrew Emigrant Aids' Societies, 6 J. 5*d* and *c*; 16 J. 5*d.*
Russia, Anti-Jewish Disturbances in, 10 A. 3*f*; 14 A. 5*c*; 15 A. 7*e*; 19 A. 7*d*; 20 A. 5*d*; 5 M. 5*b*; 8 M. 7*e*; 18 M. 5*c.*
Russia, Anti-Semitic Disturbances in, 29 J. 5*d.*
Russia, Anti-Semitic Movement in, 18 M. 5*c.*
Russia. Case of 3 young men who in the Anti-Jewish Riot at Delossay killed a Jew—Sentence, 29 J. 5*e.*
Russia, Jews in, 15 A. 7*e*; 18 A. 5*c*; 21 A. 5*b*; 22 A. 7*a*; 24 A. 7*e*; 1 M. 5*e.*
Russia, Jews Emigrating from, 2 M. 7*d*; 6 M. 7*d*; 12 M. 5*e*; 13 M. 7*d*; 19 M. 5*d*; 20 M. 7*e*; 26 M. 5*c*; 26 J. 6*a.*
Russia, Jews, Official Circular Forbidding, 24 J. 7*d.*
Russia, Jews Expelled from, 28 A. 5*e.*
Russia, Jews invited by Circular to join the Nihilists, 28 A. 5*e.*
Russian Jews, Official Regulations concerning, 25 M. 7*e.*
Russian Jews, Persecution of, 19 A. 8*a*; 1 M. 5*c*; 8 M. 7*e*; 26 M. 5*e.*
Russia and the Powers, 6 M. 7*b.*
Russia, Jews in, Persecution of, Trials resulting from, to be called Urgent, 24 A. 7*e.*
Russian Jews in United States, Despatches on, 4 M., 7*d*; 6 M. 7*b.*
Russia. Jewish Apothecaries forbidden in St. Petersburg, 5 A. 5*c.*
Russia. Jewish Surgeons not to act in the Army, 10 J. 7*f.*
Trial and Sentences on Anti-Jewish rioters, 30 J. 5*c.*
Russian Jewish refugees in London, 4 A. 10*f.*

3rd Quarter : July—Sept.

Jews, Prosecution of, in Russia, Meeting of the Relief Fund at the Mansion House, 27 July 6*e*; 22 Aug. 8*b*; 25 Sept. 6*d*; 22 Sept. 8*b.*

Newspapers—England—London—*continued.*

The Times, 1882—continued.
Jews, Contributions to aid, 26 Aug. 11*e.*
Jews, General Drentch's Speech to the Deputation of, at
  Balta, 6 Sept. 3*d.*
Jews and the Grain Trade, 8 Sept. 8*f.*
Jews in the United States, 8 Sept. 6*c.*
Russia, Trial of Anti-Jewish rioters, 30 Aug. 5*d.*
Russian Commerce and the Jews, 1 Sept. 4*f.*
Russo-Jewish Refugees Fund, 4 July, 11*b.*

4th Quarter : Oct.—Dec.

Jews in Russia, Persecution of, Meeting of the Mansion
  House Fund for the Relief of Sufferers, 28 Oct. 4*d.*
Russia, Anti-Jewish Rioters, Sentences on, 4 Dec. 5*f.*
Trial of the Anti-Jewish Rioters, 9 Oct. 3*e* ; 17 Oct. 5*c.*

1883.

Austria, Trial of Prisoners for Plundering Houses of
  Jews, 19 Oct. 3*c.*
Criminal Trials, Jews for the Murder of a Christian Girl,
  [Tisza Eszlar], 20 June 7*b* and *c* ; 21 June 5*c* and *e* ;
  22, 5*c* ; 23, 7*d* ; 25, 5*d* ; 26, 5*b* ; 27, 5*c* ; 29, 5*c* ; 3
  July, 5*c* ; 7 July, 7*b* ; 9, 7*c* ; 12, 5*c* ; 13, 5*c* ; 14, 7*c* ;
  16, 5*f* ; 17, 7*d* ; 18, 7*d* ; 19, 5*e* ; 20, 5*c* ; 21, 7*d* ; 23,
  5*f* ; 24, 5*c* ; 25, 5*d* ; 26, 5*d* ; 28, 5*c* ; 30, 5*e* ; 31, 5*a* ;
  1 August, 5*c* ; 2, 5*b* ; 4, 5*b* ; 6, 5*e.*
Criminal Trials, Appeal dismissed, 24 Dec. 5*e.*
Criminal Trials, Dr. H. Adler on, 5 July, 9*e.*
Criminal Trials, Note on, 4 Aug. 4*f.*
Criminal Trials, Leaders on, 10 July 9*f* ; 4 Aug. 9*e.*
Hungary, Anti-Jewish Disturbances in, 20 Aug. 5*f* ; 28
  Aug. 5*d* ; 29 Aug. 3*c* ; 5 Sept. 5*c.*
Hungary, Anti-Semitic Club formed in. 28 Sept. 3*c.*
Hungary, Anti-Semitic Parliamentary Club formed in, 15
  Oct. 6*a.*
Hungary, Jewish monuments in cemetery destroyed in,
  24 Aug. 3*c.*
Jewesses, Flogging of, at Casablanca, 30 March, 10*d.*
Jewish Colony in Palestine, 4 Sept. 7*f* ; 8 Dec. 5*d.*
Jewish Colony in America, New Odessa in Oregon, 2
  Aug. 10*e.*

Newspapers—England—London—*continued.*

The Times, 1883—continued.
Leading Articles—Herr Stöcker in London, 13 Dec. 9*c*
Leading Articles—Jews in Russia, 17 Aug. 7*c.*
Leading Articles—Hungarian Trials, 10 July, 9*f*; 4 Aug. 9*e.*
Russia, Anti-Jewish riots in, 5 Sept. 3*d* ; 8 Sept. 5*e* ; 12 Oct. 5*d* ; 13, 5*c.*
Russia, Anti-Semitic disorders, 12 Sept. 5*a* ; 29 Oct. 4*d* ; 12 Nov. 6*a.*
Russia, Excesses against Jews, 1 Oct. 6*a* ; 8 Oct. 5.
Russia, Excesses in Pesth [*sic !*], 9 Aug. 5*e*; 27 Sept. 3*c.*
Russia, Expulsion of English Jews from, 16 Aug. 6*b* ; 22 Aug. 5*a.*
Russia, Jewish Distillers forbidden in, 28 Aug. 5*b.*
Russia, Jewish Manufacturers forbidden to employ Christian labourers, 16 Aug. 7*d.*
Russia, Jews in, State of, 23 July, 6*b* ; 31 Aug. 3*d.*
Russia, M. Cremieux's Document, Appeal to the Jews in, 22 Nov. 5*b.*
Russia, Riots at Rastof, 6 Aug. 5*e.*
Russia, Riots at Riga, 27 Aug. 3*b.*
Stöcker, Herr—Calumny on the venerable Sir Moses Montefiore, 1 Dec. 5*c.*
Stöcker, Herr—Correspondence about him as an Anti-Jewish agitator, 12 Nov. 6*b* ; 13 Nov. 7*b.*
Stöcker, Herr—Letter about his Lecture at the Mansion House, 9 Nov. 6*f.*
Stöcker, Herr—Specimens of Jew-baiting Addresses on his return to Berlin, 1 Dec. 5*c.*
Stöcker, Herr—Baron de Worms resigns his membership of the St. Stephen's Club from his Lecture there, 26 Nov. 5*d* ; 29 Nov. 9*a.*

Newspapers—France—Paris.

333. L'Anti-Juif. 1882. **A.**

[Only three numbers appeared ; said only to have been bought by Jews.]

333a. Le péril social, 1884. **A.**

[Weekly. Successor to *L'Anti-Semitique,* No. 334.]

Newspapers—France—Montdidier.

334. L'Anti-Semitique. 1883. **A.**
[? Weekly. Only 10 Nos. appeared.]

334a. *La Tribune Philosemitique.* **P.**
[Weekly. Editor, Gaetan Rossetti. Only 3 Nos. appeared commencing Wednesday, 2nd October, 1883.]

Newspapers—Germany. *Cf.* Broadsheets, 111-2.

Prof. Bresslau (No. 107) gives the following account of the rise of the Anti-Semitic movement in the German press, 1875.

July.—*Kreuzzeitung,* 5 Aera Artikeln (= No. 13) [Evangelical conservative.]

Aug.—*Germania* [Conservative-ultramontane.] *Deutsche Eisenbahnzeitung* [afterwards *Reichsglocke.*] *Deutsche Landes-Zeitung* [Agrarian.]

Sept.—*Oesterreichisher Volksfreund, Bairischer Kurier, Bavaria, Augsburger Postzeitung, Badischer Beobachter, Mainzer Journal, Fuldaer Ztg., Kölnische Volks Ztg., Düsseldorfer Volksblatt, Essener Blätter, Wupperthaler Volksblätter, Köln-Bergheimer Ztg.* [All 12 ultramontane.] *Staatsbürger Ztg.* [ultra-radical.] *Neue Freie Ztg.* [do.] *Dresdener Reichszeitung* [particularist.]

Oct.—*Ratibor Leobschützer Ztg.* [ultramontane.]

Nov.—*Reichsbote* [conservative.]

Newspapers—Germany—Berlin.

335. Berliner Ostend Zeitung. **A.**
[Daily, 1881.]

336. Deutsches Tageblatt. Grosses Conservatives-Organ.
[1881, Daily.] **A.**

337. Der Reichsherold. Einziges freisinniges national-deutsches (anti-semitisches) Organ. **A.**
[Biweekly, 1881, editor Dr. E. Henrici. *cf.* Posters, 395-6.]

Newspapers – Germany – Cassel.

338. Reichsgeldmonopol. Organ für social-politische Reform. **A.**
[Weekly, 1882.]

Newspapers—Germany—Dresden.

339. Deutsche Reform. Organ der antijüdischen deutsch-nationalen Reformpartei. **A.**
[Weekly, Dec. 1879—Dec. 1880, biweekly, 1 Jan. 1881, daily from 1 April, 1882.]

Newspapers—Germany—Liegnitz.

340. Patriotische Zeitung. Antijüdisches Organ. **A.**
[Weekly, 1881.]

Newspapers—Germany—Mainz.

341. Die Wucherpille. Anti-semitisches Organ. 1882.
[Weekly.] **A.**

Newspapers—Germany—Würzburg.

342. Der Anti-Semit. 1881. **A.**
[Weekly ? Editor imprisoned for an article inciting Christians to attack the Jews—June, 1881.]

Newspapers—Roumania—Bucharest.

342a. Emigrantul. 1883, in progress. **P.**
[Biweekly. Editor, L. Rokeat; in Judæo-German printed in square Hebrew characters. For information of those leaving Roumania.]

Niendorf, M. A.

343. Denkschrift über die vier "invaliden" Fonds des deutschen Reichs. Eine Sammlung von actenmässigen parliamentarischen wie bankokratischen Materials zur Geschichte der pecuniären Lage dieser Fonds von 1873–1876. Berlin, 1877 (M. A. Niendorf.) 8vo. pp. 2 + 176. [9. Die Judenfrage im Reichstag, p. 110-14.] **A.**

Nobel, Rabbiner Josef.

344. Kritisches Richtschwert für Rohling's "Talmudjude," eine quellengemässe strengkritische Beurtheilung des obengenannten Buches, zu Nutz und Frommen ehrlich denkender Christen und Juden. Totis (Ungarn) 1881 (Meyer). 8vo. pp. iii. and 86 and i. **P.**
[Reprinted from *Jüdische Presse;* to be followed by a second part.]

Norton, Richard.

345. Die Epoche der Begriffsverwirrung. Zweite Auflage. Berlin, 1881 (Steinitz). 8vo. pp. 84. **P.**

Observator [pseud.]

345a. Magyarország vágtaloa Frohamos elszegenyedése vallás talanzaga es mezsidosodása. [Hungary's rapid impoverishment, irreligion and Judaization.] Zombor, 1880. 8vo. pp. 32 (K). **A.**

Official Papers—England—Houses of Parliament.

346. Principalities No. 1, 1877. Correspondence respecting the Condition and Treatment of the Jews in Servia and Roumania. fol. pp. 359 [mostly reproduced (in French) in Loeb, No. 284.]

347. Russia No. 3 (1881). Correspondence respecting the expulsion of Mr. L. Lewisohn. fol. pp. 18.

348. Russia No. 4 (1881) ditto. In continuation of Russia, No. 3 (1881). fol. pp. 29.

349. Russia, No. 1, 1882. Correspondence respecting the Treatment of Jews in Russia. London, 1882 (Harrison and Sons.) 8vo. pp. i. (precis) and 27 [containing 21 communications from and to the British Embassy at St. Petersburg and from Consuls in Russia, from May 16, 1881, to Jan. 25, 1882.]

350. Russia, No. 2, 1882. In continuation of Russia No. 1, 1882.

Official Papers—France.

351. Affaires etrangères. Documents diplomatiques. Question de la reconnaissance de la Roumanie. Paris. Impr. nation. 1880. 4to. pp. 40.

351a. ——————— suite. 1880. 4to. pp. 21.

351b. Affaires etrangères. Documents diplomatiques. Question de la protection diplomatique et consulaire au Maroc. Paris, 1880 (Impr. nat.) 4to. pp. 278.
[pp. 52, 142, 171, 172, 188, 241-2, 250-4 refer to Morocco Jews.]

Official Papers—Roumania.

315c. Documente oficiale din correspondinta diplomatica de la 2/14 sept. 1878, pana la 17/29 julie, 1880. Bucharest, 1880. 8vo. pp. 242.

Official Papers—United States—House of Representatives.

352.—Condition of Israelites in Russia. Message from the President of the United States. Ex. Doc. No. 102, ordered to be printed May 2, 1882. 8vo. pp. 72 [containing 40 communications from and to the U.S. embassy at St. Petersburg. From Sept. 29, 1872 to April 15, 1882.]

Oliphant, Lawrence.

353. The Land of Gilead. London, 1881 (Blackwood) v. J. Singer. No. 480. **P.**

354. The Jews and the Eastern Question, in *Nineteenth Century.* Aug. 1882, pp. 242—255. **P.**

355. Jewish Tales and Jewish Reform, in *Blackwood's Magazine,* Nov. 1882. **P**

Onody, Geza von (Reichstags-Abgeordneter).

355a. Tisza-Eszlar in der Vergangenheit und Gegenwart. Autorisirte Uebersetzung aus dem Ungarischen von Georg von Marczianyi. Budapest, 1883 (Grimm). 8vo. pp. xiv. and 215. **A.**

[With Portrait of Esther Solymosi and reproduction of an old broadsheet.]

Oort, Prof. H.

355b. Der Ursprung der Blutbeschuldigung gegen die Juden. Vortrag beim 6 Orientalisten-Congress. Leyden, 1883 (Doesburgh). 8vo. pp. 31. **P.**

Oppenheimer, Moses.

356. Offener Brief an Herrn Adolph Stöcker, Hofprediger und Mitglied des Oberkirchenraths in Berlin. Mannheim (Selbstverlag) n.d. Zweite Auflage. [October, 1879.] 16mo. pp. 14. **P.**

357. Semiten und Arier. Zweiter Brief an Herrn Adolph Stöcker. Zweite Auflage. Mannheim (Sebstverlag). [Februar, 1880.] 12mo. pp. 15. **P.**

358. Stöcker und Treitschke in *Gegenwart,* 1880, Nos. 1 and 2, pp. 71 seq. [H. B. xx. 33.] **P.**

Parliamentary Reports—England.

359. *Hansard's Parliamentary Debates.* Third Series. Vol. cclxvi. Russia, Persecution of the Jews. Question, Observations, the Duke of Somerset. Reply, Earl Granville, short debates thereon Feb. 9, 1882 (House of Lords), p. 225. Questions, Mr. W. H. James, Mr. Serjeant Simon. Answers, Sir Charles W. Dilke, Mr. Gladstone, p. 244. Question, Baron Henry de Worms. Answers Mr. Gladstone, Feb. 13, 1882, p. 503. Questions, Viscount Folkestone, Baron Henry de Worms; Answers Sir Charles W. Dilke, Feb. 20th, 1882, p. 1102.

[See *Christian and Jew*, Newspapers, No. 330a.]

Hansard's Parliamentary Debates. Third Series. Vol. cclxvii. Debate on motion of Baron Henry de Worms, "That this House, deeply deploring the persecution and outrages to which the Jews have been subjected in portions of the Russian Empire, trusts that her Majesty's Government will find means, either alone or in conjunction with other great Powers, of using their good offices with the Government of His Majesty the Czar to prevent the recurrence of similar acts of violence." 3rd March, 1882, col. 30-70. Speakers: Baron Henry de Worms, col. 30-37; Mr. J. Slagg, 38-40; Mr. Serjt. Simon, 40-45 (ruled out of order, p. 44); Mr. Gladstone, 45-51; Sir Stafford Northcote, 52-54; Mr. O'Donnell, 55-57; Mr. Arthur Cohen, 57-59; Mr. Bourke, 59-60; Mr. Ecroyd, 60-61; Sir Charles W. Dilke, 61-4; Mr. Ashmead Bartlett, 64-68; Mr. Warton, 68-9; Mr. E. Collins, 69-70; Mr. R. N. Fowler, 70.

Hansard's Parliamentary Debates. Third Series. Vol. cclxviii. Questions, Baron Henry de Worms. Answers, Sir Charles W. Dilke, March 27th, 1882, col. 23; April 27, col. 1559; May 1, col. 1817.

Parliamentary Reports—Prussia.

360. Einige Erklärungen über die Judenfrage aus früheren Sitzungen des Preussischen Herrenhauses. Abdruck aus den stenographischen Berichten. Berlin, 1880 (Heinicke). 8vo. pp. 40.

Parliamentary Reports—Prussia—*continued.*

361. Die Judenfrage vor dem Preussischen Landtage. Wortgetreuer Abdruck der Verhandlungen im Abgeordnetenhause am 20 u. 22 Nov. 1880. Berlin, 1880 (Steinitz). 8vo. pp. 124.

362. Der Fall Kantorowicz und die Judenfrage vor dem Preussischen Abgeordnetenhause am 20 u. 22 Nov. 1880. Abdruck der an die Interpellation Hänel geknüpten Reden ; nach dem amtlichen Bericht, nebst einem Sprechregister und der Petition an den Reichskanzler. Zweite Auflage. Berlin, 1881 (A. Werckenthin).

363. Die Judenfrage. Verhandlungen des Preussischen Abgeordnetenhauses über die Interpellation des Abgeordneten Dr. Hänel, am 20 u. 22 Nov. 1882. Separatabdruck der Amtlichen Stenographischen Berichte des Hauses der Abgeordneten. Berlin, 1880 (W. Moeser). 8vo. pp. 211.

364. Contra Stöcker. Drei Reden der Abgeordneten Löwe (Berlin), Stöcker, Hänel gehalten in der Sitzung des preussischen Abgeordnetenhauses vom 11 Februar, 1880. Berlin, 1880 (C. Barthel). 8vo. pp. 16.

365. Stenographischer Bericht. Haus der Abgeordneten. Zwanzigste Sitzung, am 25 Februar, 1882. 4to. double cols. pp. 483–515. [Speakers : Stöcker, Virchow, v. Puttkamer, Strosser, E. Richter, Cremer, Schröder, Graf Clairon D'Haussonville. After end of discussion, personal explanations by Berger, Virchow, Stöcker, Richter, Schröder, Cremer.]

Parliamentary Reports—Roumania.

366. La Question Juive dans les Chambres Roumaines. Compte rendu des séances de la chambre des députés et du sénat du mois de mai, 1879. Publié par l'Alliance israélite universelle. Paris, 1879. (Bureau de l'Alliance). 8vo. pp. xxii. and 47.

Parliamentary Reports—Roumania—*continued.*

366a. Motionea Nerevisionistilor in Cestiunea Israelita şi cele trei discursuri ale Deputatului Colegiuliu IV. de Braila, Nicolae Blaramburg, precum şi discursurile Deputatuliu Colegiului III. de Jaşi, Conta, şi ale Deputatului Colegiului I. de Bacan, D. Rosseli Tetcanu, destinata a' i servi de commentariu. Bucaresc, 1879 (Göbl.)

[Motion of the Revisionists in the Jewish Question and the three speeches of the Deputies Blaramburg, Conta and Rosseti-Tetcanu intended to serve as a commentary on the same.]

Perinhardt, J.

367. Die deutschen Juden und W. Marr. Zweite Auflage. Loebau, 1879 (Skrzeczck). 8vo. pp. 42. **A.**

Periodicals—England—London.

The Contemporary Review, Jan. 1881.

368. The Jews in Germany, by the author of *German Home Life.* **A**

[Countess M. von Bothmer, *q. v.*]

Edinburgh Review, April, 1883.

369. Persecution of the Jews. **P.**

The Fortnightly Review, April—Aug. 1878.

370. The Political Adventures of Lord Beaconsfield. **A.**

London Quarterly Review, Oct. 1882.

371. The Jewish Question, pp. 94-119. **P.**

[Reviewing Consular Reports, Nos. 349 and 350, and Salamon, No. 449.]

National Quarterly Review, July, 1880.

371a. The Political Future of the Jews. **P.**

The Spectator.

371b. 1880, 28th Nov. Letter of P. Magnus protesting against Anti-Jewish tone.
,,   ,,   Jewish Success.

Periodicals—London—*Spectator—continued.*

1882, 14th and 21st Jan. Articles on Russian
  Jews.
  ,,   4th Feb. Mansion House Meeting.
  ,,   4th Nov. Mental Impenetrability [of Jews
     not accepting Christianity.]
1883, 23rd July. Note on Tisza-Eszlar [suggesting
     a possible sect of Thugs among Jews, cf.
     No. 17a.]
  ,,   3rd. Aug. Jew-Hatred.
  ,,   25th Aug. Why Jews are Persecuted.
  ,,   1st Nov. Letter of O. J. Simon—Jewish
     Sensitiveness.   **A.**

   The Saturday Review.

371c. The Jews in Europe. 10th Feb. 1877, 21th Aug.
     1880.
     The Jews in America. 14th July, 1877.
     Jews in Germany. 20th Nov. 1880, 27th Nov.
     1880.
     Jews in Russia. 28th May, 1881, 2nd July, 1881,
     8th July, 1882.
     Jews and Germans, 8th Jan. 1881.
     The Apologists of Jew-baiting [O. K. etc.] 14th
     Jan. 1882.
     More Jew-baiting. 1st Sept. 1883.   **P.**

   Periodicals—France—Paris. *Economiste Fran-
     çais*—June 4, 1881.

372. L'agitation anti-sémitique et le rôle economique
     des Israélites en Russie (by the St. Petersburg cor-
     respondent.)   **P.**

   Nouvelle Revue.

373. La situation en Russie. 15 Fevrier, 1882. **A.**

374. Que faire? Réponse a l'auteur de la situation en
     Russie. 15 Mai, 1882.   **P.**

Periodicals—Germany.

Allgemein, Evangel-Luther. Kirchen Zeitung.

374a. Die Stellung der Juden in Deutschland, 1876, pp. 354-7. **A.**

Das Ausland, 1880.

375. Der Judenstamm in naturhistorischer Beziehung. pp. 453 *seq.* 474 *seq.* **A.**

[Author, A. E(scherisch), refers to an earlier article on same subject.]

376. *Die Deutsche Wacht.* Monatsschrift für nationale Kulturinteressen. Organ der anti-jüdischen Vereinigung. Berlin. **A.**

[From Nov. 1879. Editor, W. Marr.]

Gewerbliche Zeitschrift herausgegeben von E. Bernhardi, 1880.

377. Das Judenthum im wirthschaftlichen und politischen Leben Deutschlands. [H.B. xx. 77.] **A.**

[Republished in *Period. Blätter zu grossen religiösen Fragen,* 1880, pp. 475-8.]

Grenzboten, 1880.

377a. Beiträge zur Beurtheilung d. Judenfrage. 7. Die polnischen Juden nochmals. p. 155. **A.**

Historisch-politische Blätter v. Görres. Band. 85. 1880, pp. 889-97.

378. Das Erstgeburtsrecht und die Stellung der Semiten in der Geschichte. [*à propos* of Lord Beaconsfield.] [H.B. xx. 77.] **A.**

379. *Der Kulturkämpfer,* herausgegeben v. Otto Glogau. Berlin, 1880. In progress. **A.**

[Fortnightly, many Anti-Jewish articles.]

Neue Evangelische Kirchenzeitung.

379a. Blicke in das heutige Judenthum, 1876, pp. 33-6, 57-9, 73-5.
Blicke in das moderne Judenthum, 1877, pp. 440, 453, 474.

Ergebnisse der antijüdischen Bewegung, 1880,
p. 420.
Die Judenfrage im Oberhause, 1881, Nov. 27. **A.**

380. *Die Wahrheit,* Humoristisch-satirisches Wochen-
blatt. **A.**
[Weekly, illustrated, 1880-2.]

Piton, Heinrich (Protest. Pfarrer).

381. Die "Judenfrage" Predigt über Math. VII. 12.
Annweiler, 1881 (Meissner u. Philippson). 12mo.
pp. 16. **P.**

Perrot.

382. Die Juden im deutschen Staats- und Volksleben.
2te Aufl. Frankfurt a-M. 1878. [H. B. xx. 33.] **A.**

Philadelphus [Pseudonym].

383. Contra Treitschke. Breslau, 1879. Separatabdruck aus der Schles. Presse, 5 Dec. [H. B. xx. 78.]
P.

Plath, Karl Heinrich Christian (Missions-
inspector.)

384. Was machen wir Christen mit unsern Juden !?
Erörtert und beantwortet. Nördlingen, 1881 (Beck).
8vo. pp. iv. and 187 and 1. **C.**

385. Welcher Stellung haben die Glieder der christlichen
Kirche dem modernen Judenthume gegenüber einzu-
nehmen? August-Conferenzvortrag. Berlin, 1881
(Sebstverlag). 12mo. pp. 38. **C.**

Platter, Prof. Dr. Julius.

385a. Der Wucher in der Bukowina. Zweite unverän-
derter Abdruck. Jena, 1878 (Fischer). 8vo. **A.**
[On Jews, pp. 41-50 giving statistics of executions by usurious
creditors, 1876-7.]

Polakowsky, Dr. H.

386. Was soll mit den Juden geschehen? Eine Anlei-
tung zur gesetzlichen Lösung der Judenfrage. Berlin,
1881 (Schulze). **A-**

[Author published in 1859, *Hundert Bogen aus über* 500 *Schriften über die Juden.*]

Porsch, J. K.

387. Kleiner Juden-Spiegel darinnen man klar und
deutlich sehen kann wie beim Viehhandel der Bauer von
den Juden schändlich betrogen wird. Neuer Abdruck
der im Jahre 1848 erschienenen und längst vergriffenen
Auflage. Schleusingen, 1880 (Glaser). 8vo. pp. 47. **C.**

Post Cards. [Intended to be sent to annoy Jews.]

388. (1). Neu Meseritz den . . . 18 . . . Jewish Pedlar
with bundle "Nach Jerusalem," and at foot "aus Russland." **A.**

(2.) Itzig's im Theater [caricature : Jewish family in
the boxes of a theatre.] **A.**

> Mit der Mischpoche geht in das Theater
> Herr Tateleben *alias* Judenvater
> Vor allen Dingen ist sein Ideal,
> Der deutsche Dichter Oscar Blumenthal.
> Weil Koscher er zu dichten gut versteht,
> Nur Knoblauchsduft durch seine Dramen weht.

Posters v. Broadsheets.

389. Royal Aquarium / The Great / Russian Waxworks /
Exhibition . . . . . Massacre of Jews at Balta. [June.
1883.]

Posters.

390. Christlich soziale / Partei / 2 Reichstag-Wahlkreis
/ Heute Dienstag den 14 Juni, Abends 8 Uhr, Oeffentliche / Versammlung im grossen Saale der / Tivoli
Brauerei / Tages-ordnung. 1. Haben Juden das Recht in
die Angelegenheiten der christlichen Kirche sich / einzu-
mischen? 2. Die Angriffe auf die christlich-soziale Partei
besonders Herrn Hofprediger Stöcker von Seiten der
Herren Dr. Langerhaus, Heckmann und Genossen . . .
(Printers, Nauck and Hartmann.) **A.**

Posters—*continued.*

391. Christlich sociale Partei / Oeffentliche / Versammlung / Donnerstag den 4 August Abends 8 Uhr im Grossen Saale der / Tivoli Brauerei / Kreuzberg / Vortrag des Landtagsabgeordneten Hofprediger Stöcker / Recht und Gerechtigkeit für Alle ! Ein Entrittsgeld zur Bestreitung der Kosten wird erbeten / J. A. Hapke. [Printers, Nauck and Hartmann.] **A.**

392. Deutsche Wähler / des Reichstagswahlkreises ! / Sonnabend den 29 October / Abends 8 Uhr / Versammlung in der Siegessaüle / Referent : / Herr Liebermann von Sonnenberg / Thema : / Warum hat der Jude dies mal noch / gesiegt ? / Deutsche Gegner willkommen Juden in ihrem / eigenen Interesse ausgeschlossen. (Gedruckt bei Julius Ruppel.) **A.**

393.

Kandidat
der Juden-Juden
Genossen
ist der jüdische Gründer
Ludwig Loewe.

Kandidat.
der
Christlichen Deutschen
ist der Premier-Lieutenant der
Landwehr Herr
Max Liebermann
von Sonnenberg,
Ritter des eisernen Kreuzes.

[Printer, Julius Ruppel.] **A.**

394. II. Reichstags-Wahlkreis / Versammlung / antifortschrittlicher-Wahlmänner / des unterzeichneten Stadtbezirkes / Donnerstag den 29 September, Abends 8 Uhr in / Th. Keller's Hof-Jäger) Hasenhaide / Tages-Ordnung : Vortrag der / Herren Dr. Bernhard Förster / Die Stellung des Arbeiter zu den bevorstehenden Reichstagswahlen / Die antifortschritlichen Wahlvorstände der Stadtbezirke, 56a. bis 60, 77, 80, 81. (Printers, Nauck and Hartmann.)

395. Der / Reichsherold / Redacteur : / Dr. Ernst Henrici/ Einziges freisinniges national- / deutsches (anti-semitisches) Organ / erscheint zweimal wöchentlich Mittwochs und Sonnabends. (Printers, Nauck and Hartmann.) **A.**

Posters—*continued.*

396. Der Reichsherold / Redacteur / Dr. Ernst Henrici-
enthält / in der heutigen Nummer / der grosse / Stein.
Diebstahl / verübt an städtischem Eigenthum /   . . .
(Printers, Nauck and Hartmann.)   **A.**

397. Sociale / Reichsverein / Heute / Dienstag den 17
Mai, 1881, in der / Tonhalle / Friedrich-strasse 112 /
Oeffentliche / Versammlung / Referent : / Dr. Ernst
Henrici / Ueber die brennendsten socialen und nationalen
Tagesfragen / Der Zutritt ist nur Deutschen Männern
gestattet / Zur Deckung der Kosten Entrée nach Belieben.
(Printers, Nauck and Hartmann.)   **A.**

398. Socialer Reichverein / Montag / den 25 Juli
Abends 8½ Uhr / bei Buggenhagen, Montzplatz / Oeffent-
liche / Versammlung / Referent / Dr. Ernst Henrici /
Politik und Religion / Jeder freisinniger deutscher Bürger
ist eingeladen / Zur Deckung der Kosten Entrée nach
Belieben. (Nauck and Hartmann.)   **A.**

399. Sociales / Reichsverein / Mittwoch den 3 August,
Abends 8½ Uhr findet in Köhler's Saal / Ecke der
Teltower und Möckemstrasse eine / Oeffentliche Ver-
sammlung / statt / Herr Dr. Ernst Henrici / wird über
das Thema " Was verscheucht die Berliner von der /
Wahlurne? " sprechen / Alle fresinnigen Bürger deutschen
Stammes sind eingeladen / Zur Deckung der Kosten ein
kleines Entrée nach Belieben / Der Vorstand. (Printers,
Nauck and Hartmann.)   **A.**

400. Soeben erschienen und ist hier zu haben : / Die
Situation. / Erste Extrafahrt der " Dampfwatze " /
Inhalt / 1. Die Entstehung des Konservativ-antisemitischen Bündnisses / . . . . . 4. Die Berichtigung
der antisemitischen Idee / 5. Konservative Drohungen
oder Fürchtet euch nicht vor'm schwarzen Mann ! / Gross
8vo. Broschirt. Preis 30 pf. . . . Commissionsverlag
von Oscar Lorenz in Berlin.   **A.**
(Printer, Baensch, cf. Wasinski, No. 517.)

Posters—*continued*.

401. Theaterfreunde / Berlins! / Der Redacteur des "Apollo," Herr Louis Cunow, / hält heut Abend 8½ Uhr im / Deutschen Vereinshause Wilhelmstr. 118 / einen Vortrag. / Thema / "Wie ist das deutsche Theater zu heben und welche Mittel / und Wege sind einzuschlagen um den unlauteren Treiben / der Herren Theater-Agenten u. Directoren Einhalt zu thun" / Nur Herren und *Damen* deutscher Abkunft ist der Eintritt gestattet da es sich um eine echt / deutsche Sache handelt. (Printed by Nauck u. Hartmann.)   **A.**

Protest.

402. "Erklärung" against the Anti-Semitic movement signed by 80 notabilities including Gneist, Mommsen, Siemens, Virchow, and Zeller, appeared in Berlin newspapers, 14 Nov. 1879.   **P.**

[Given in *Kehraus*, No. 124, p. 42.]

Pseudonyms.

See *Amitti, Amyntor, Austriacus, Barine, Beta, Chevalier, Eliot, Enodatus, Germanicus, Gladius, Hutten, Judäus, Junius, Jurisconsultus, Justus, Kühn, Leib, Lindauer, Ludolf, M. Gy., M. J. H., Marr II., Molchow, Naudh, Neofito, Observator, Philadelphus, R. Th., Rauchmann, Rubens, Sagittarius, Sailer, Sanders, Simplex, Simplicissimus, Sulpicius, V.C.P., Valbert.*

R. Th.

403. Was ist es mit der Judenfrage? Ein Kurzes Wort zur Belehrung und Beherzigung. Neustettin, 1881 (Kielich). 12mo. pp. 13.   **P.**

Ragozin, Madame Z.

404. Russian Jews and Gentiles from a Russian point of view. In *Century Magazine*, April 1882, pp. 905-920.   **A.**

[Mainly founded on Brafmann, No. 106, answered by Miss Emma Lazarus, No. 271.]

Rahlenbeck, A.

405. Le mouvement antijuif à Berlin. In *Revue de Belgique*, 15th March, 1880. **P.**

Railway Ticket.

405a. With inscription "Nach Jerusalem. Kein Retour-Billet," to be sent to Jews. **A.**

Rauchmann, Leo. (= Rabbiner, J. Stern.)

406. Die Mischehe zwischen Juden und Christen. Mit einem Anhang : Der ächte Ring. Zürich, 1881 (Schabelitz). **P.**

407. Religiöse Scheidewände. Ein Wink in der Juden-verfolgung. Zürich, 1881 (Schabelitz). 12mo. pp. 32. **P.**

Reichenbach, A.

408. Nach der Hatz. Kritische Betrachtung der letzten Judenhetze in Deutschland als die neueste Krankheits-erscheinung des deutschen Volkes. Zürich, 1881 (Schabelitz). 8vo. pp. i. and 67. **P.**

Report—Jewish Societies. [cf. Compte-rendus, Nos. 142-5.]

409. Anglo-Jewish Association. Annual Report. Sixth —Thirteenth. 1876-1884.
[By Rev. A. Löwy.]

410. Bulletins de l'Alliance israélite Universelle. Deux-ième Série, Sept. 1880. In progress. Paris: Siége de la Société, 1880-4.
[By M. Isidore Loeb.]

410a. Hebrew Emigrants' Aid Society of the United States. Report of Moritz Ellinger. New York, 1882. 8vo. pp. 33.
[On his journey to Europe to confer with chief European Jews, letters from whom are attached, pp. 25-33.]

73

Report—Jewish Societies—*continued*.

411. Jahresbericht der israelitischen Allianz zu Wien, 1875—1884 (Nos. 2-11). In Progress. Vienna.

411a. Mittheilungen des Press-Ausschusses des Comités zur Unterstützung der bedrängten russischen Israeliten zu Frankfurt am Main (1882).

412. Mittheilungen vom deutsch-israelitischen Gemeindesbunde. Berlin.

412a. Monatsbericht des Deutschen Central-Comités für die russisch-jüdischen Flüchtlinge (from May, 1882.)

Reports —Meetings.

412b. Central Comité zur Erleichterung der Auswanderung der Israeliten aus Rumänien. II. General-Versammlung einberufen am 4/16 und 5/17 Sept. 1883, zu Galatz. Galatz, 1883 (J. Schene). 8vo. pp. 72. **P.**

413. Denkschrift nebst den dazu gehörigen Referaten für die erste General-Versammlung der Social-conservativen Vereinigung zu Berlin am 18 u. 19 Mai, 1881. Herausgegeben von dem Bureau des provisorischen Vorstandes. Berlin, 1881 (M. Schultze). 8vo. pp. ii. and 159. **A.**

414. Die Fälschung der öffentlichen Meinung nachgewiesen durch den stenographischen Bericht über die erste öffentliche Sitzung der neubegründeten Deutschen Volksvereins am 14 März, 1881, im grossen Concert-Saale der Tivoli-Aktien-Brauerei. Herausgegeben vom Vorstande des Deutschen Volksvereins. Berlin, 1881 (Luckhardt). 8vo. pp. 47. **A.**
[45-47, Statuten des Vereins. Vorsitzender : Dr. Bernhard Förster.]

415. Die öffentliche Feier des dritten Stiftungsfestes des fortschrittlichen Vereins "Waldeck" am 10 Januar, 1881, im Concertsaale der Reichshallen. Stenographischer Bericht von Julius Weiss. Berlin 1881 (Barthel). 8vo. pp. 31. **P.**

Reports—Meetings—*continued*.

415a. Proceedings of the Conference of Hebrew Emigrants' Aid Society and Auxiliary Committees, representing the various cities of the United States and Canada, at New York, June 4th, 1882. New York, 1882 (Davis). 8vo. pp. 22. **P.**

416. Die studentische Petition als Annex der allgemeinen Petition betreffend die Einschränkung der jüdischen Machtstellung. Ein Beitrag zur Orientriung über Gründe und Zwecke derselben. Zweite und vermehrte (Doppel) Auflage. Leipzig, 1881 (Frohberg). 8vo. pp. 32. **A.**
[Eight speeches by various students, 22 Nov. and 10 Dec. 1881.]

417. Die Verurtheilung der antisemitischen Bewegung durch die Wahlmänner von Berlin. Bericht über die allgemeine Versammlung der Wahlmänner aus den vier Berliner Landtags-Wahlkreisen am 12 Jan. 1881, im oberen Saale der Reichshallen. Berlin, 1881 (G. Bartel). 8vo. pp. 16. **A.**

Reports. Russian Refugees.

418. Bericht über die Bildung der ersten Niederlassung russischer Juden in den Vereinigten Staaten zu Catahoula Parish, Louisiana, erstattet von dem Verein zur Beförderung israelitischen Auswanderer nach den Vereinigten Staaten, in New York. Aus dem Englischen übersetzt. Frankfurt a/M., 1882 (J. Kauffmann). 8vo. pp. 16. **P.**
[Signed " J. Stanwood Menken, President."]

Reports. Russia.

418a. Rapport de la Delegation de Zemstvo (Conseil Général) d'Odessa sur la question juive. Odessa, 1881.
[Referred to *Edin. Rev.* Ap. 1883.] **A.**

Reppert, Prof. Dr. Joseph. [? Rebbert.]

419. Christenschutz nicht Judenhatz. Ein Volksbüchlein 4 Auf. Paderborn, 1879. 8vo. pp. 32. (H. B. xxi. 51.) **A.**

Reppert, Prof. Dr. J.—*continued.*

420. Blicke in's Talmudische Judenthum. Nach den For-
schungen von Dr. Konrad Martin, Bischof v. Paderborn,
dem christlichen Volke enthüllt. Nebst einer Beleuchtung der neuesten Judenvertheidigung. Paderborn, 1879.
8vo. pp. 96. **A.**

Renan, Ernest.

421. L'Ecclesiaste. Paris, 1882. C. Levy. **A,**
[Preface first appeared in *Revue des deux Mondes.* A protest
against the want of idealism in Modern Jews.]

422. Letter to Rabbi of Szanto on Blood Accusation
in Hungary. **P.**
[Given in *Revue des Etudes juives,* Jan. 1883.]

423. Le Judaisme comme Race et comme Religion. Paris,
1883. (C. Levy.) 8vo. pp. 26. **P.**
[Translated into German and into Roumanian.]

Reuss, Rod.

423a. L'Affaire de Tisze-Eszlar, un episode de l'histoire
de l'antisemitisme au dix-neuvième siècle. Strassburg,
1883 (Trenthal). 8vo. pp. 53. **P.**
[Extract from *Progrès religieuse.*]

Revel, Wilhelm.

424. Der Wahrheit die Ehre. Ein Beitrag zur Judenfrage in Deutschland. Nürnberg, 1881 (Wörlim). 16mo.
pp. 30. **P.**

Rhyn, Dr. Otto Henne-Am.

425. Culturgeschichte des Judenthums von den ältesten
Zeiten bis zur Gegenwart. Bern, 1880 (Costenoble). **A.**
[Adapted from Graetz, with Anti-Semitic interpretation.]

Richard, A. C.

426. Der Jüdische Specialarzt, genannt der Scheene
Isidor mit der weissen Cravatte. In *Schlesiche Volkszeitung,* 25 Jan. 1880. **A.**

Richard, G.

427. Le peuple juif : histoire et mœurs. In *Biblio-graphie universelle et révue suisse,* March and April, 1882. **A.**
[Reviewing Andrée.]

Richter, Eugen (Radical German M.P.).

428. Rede gehalten beim Feste des Fortschrittlichen Wahlvereins im 2. Berlin Reichstag-Wahlkreise am 15 August, 1881. (Printed by L. Ullstein.) Broadsheet 4to. pp. 4. **P.**

Ritter, Dr. I. H. (Prediger der jüd. Reformge-meinde).

429. Das Urbild religiösen Neides und Hasses. Homilie über 1 Buch Mose, Kap. 4 v. 1–10, gehalten am 19 October, 1879. Berlin, 1880 (Peiser). 8vo. pp. 8. **P.**

430. Wir Juden. Rede am Neujahrstage. Berlin, 1881 (Stuhr). 8vo. pp. 16. **P.**

Rizu-Lambru.

430a. O Opinione asupra Darei Drepturilor Politice si lameutenesci Israelitor din Orient (România). Bucarest. 8vo. pp. 14. **A.**
[Opinion on the granting political and civil rights to the Jews in the East (Roumania).]

Reymond, M.

431. Wo steckt der Mauschel ? oder Jüdischer Liberal-ismus und wissenschaftlicher Pessimismus. Ein offener Brief an W. Marr. Vierte Auflage. Berne and Leipzig, 1880 (Frobeen). 8vo. pp. 62. **A.**

Rodkinson, M. L.

431a. *L'baqer Mishpaṭ.* Kritischer Ueberblick (a) über den Judenspiegelprozess in Münster (10 Dec. 1883) (b) Verhandlung der Berliner Repräsentanten d. jüd. Ge-meinde wegen Erbbegräbnisspetition auf jüd. Friedhof von einem Mischeheling, Ehemann einer Jüdin (23 Dec. 1883). Berlin (Löwy), 1884. 8vo. pp. 52. **P.**
[In Hebrew.]

Rodkinson, M. L.—*continued.*

431b. Der Schulchan Aruch und seine Beziehungen zu
den Juden und Nicht-Juden. Wien, 1884 (Löwy). 8vo.
pp. 68 and x.   **P.**
[Translation of passages referring to Gentiles.]

432. Das ungesäuerte Brod und die Anklage des Blutge-
brauchs am Passah-Feste. (Pressburg) Vienna, 1883 (D.
Löwy). 8vo. pp. xiii. and 32.   **P.**
[Hebrew with German preface vii. & viii. and Hebrew letter
from S. Rubin.]

Rohan, Karl J.

433. Eine Ansicht über die Ursachen der Judenfrage
und über das Mittel zur Lösung derselben. Leipzig,
1882 (O. Wigand). 8vo. pp. 27.   **A.**

Rocholl, Dr. Heinrich.

434. Ueber die Stellung der Evangelischen Christen zur
sogenannten Judenfrage der Gegenwart. Ein Vortrag.
Köln, 1881 (Roemke). 8vo. pp. 41.   **A.**

Rohling, Prof. Dr. Aug.

435. Franz Delitzsch und die Judenfrage. Antwortlich
beleuchtet. Prag, 1881 (Reinitzer). 8vo. pp. 155. **A.**

436. Der Talmudjude. Zur Beherzigung für Juden und
Christen aller Stände dargestellt. 5 Auflage. Münster,
1876 (Rusell). 8vo. pp. 112.   **A.**

437. Meine Antworten an die Rabbiner oder : Fünf Briefe
über den Talmudismus und das Blut-ritual der Juden.
Prag, 1883 (Zeman). 8vo. pp. 106.   **A.**

437a. Polemik und Menschenopfer des Rabbinismus.
Prag, 1883.   **A.**

Roi, J. de le (Pastor in Breslau).

438. Israel, sonst jetzt und einst. Vortrag gehalten auf der
Pastoral Conferenz in Berlin am 26 Mai, 1880. Berlin,
1880. (Verlag d. Dutsch. Evang. Tractat-Gesellschaft.)
8vo. pp. 34.   **C.**

Roi, J. de le—*continued.*

438a. Die evangelische Christenheit und die Juden unter
dem Gesichtspunkte der Mission geschichtlich betrachtet.
Erster Band. Leipzig, 1884 (Reuther). 8vo. pp. xvi.
and 440. **C.**

[Preface antagonistic. History of Conversionists to 1750.
Extract published separately with title *Das Institutum judaicum
im vorigen Jahrhundert.*]

Rosenberg, Rabbiner Dr. A.

439. Das Judenthum und die Nationalitätsiden. Eine
völkerpsychologische Studie. Vienna, Kaposvar, 1882
(Pestes). 8vo. pp. 31. **P.**

Rosetti-Fezcano, D.

440. La Roumanie et le Juif devant l'Europe. Bacau,
1878. 8vo. pp. 78. (H. B. xviii. 88). **A.**

Rost L. (freiprotest, Pfr. in Alzay).

441. Zur Berufsthätigkeit der Juden gegen den Vorwurf
ihrer Arbeitsscheu. Alzey, 1880 (Weiss). 8vo. pp. 56.
P.

Rothe, Emil.

442. Die Judenfrage. Cincinnati (U. S.), 1881. 8vo.
pp. 16. (H. B. xxi. 52.) **P.**

Rubens, Dr. Wilhelm. (= Rabbiner J. Stern.)

443. Der alte und der neue Glaube im Judenthum.
Kritische Streiflichter über die Religion Israels, nebst
einem Anhang über den Talmud. Zürich, 1878 (Schabelitz). **? P.**

Rudoll, A.

444. אגרת מתוחה. Offenes Sendschreiben von A.
Freiherr v. Rothschild in Wien an Hofprediger Stöcker
in Berlin. Uebersetzt in's Hebraische. Pressburg, 1880
(Löwy u. Alkalay). 8vo. pp. 15. **P.**

[Right Hebrew, left German.]

Rülf, Rabbiner Dr. J.

444a. Amchas Bas Ammi. Israels Heilung. Ein ernstes Wort an Glaubens- und Nichtglaubens-genossen. Frankfurt a/M. 1883 (Kauffman). 8vo. pp. ii. and 94. **P.**
[With a letter to author of " Autoemancipation," No. 16, instead of preface.]

445. Drei Täge in Jüdisch-Russland. Ein Cultur- und Sittenbild. Frankfurt a/M. 1882 (Kauffmann). 8vo. pp. 131. **P.**

Ruppel, Julius.

446. Rede gehalten am 10 August im "Universum" von dem von den vereinigten antifortschrittlichen Parteien für den sechsten Berliner Reichstags, Walkreis (Norden) aufgestellten alleinigen antifortschrittlichen Candidaten Redacteur Julien Ruppel in Berlin. Newspaper. 4to. 2 pp. 3 cols. **A.**

Sagittarius (pseudonym).

447. Franz Liszt über die Juden (1881, Pesther Buchdruckerei Gesellschaft). 12mo. p. 38. **A.**
[Extracting and reviewing *Les Bohemiens et de leur musique en Hongrie* par F. Liszt.]

Sailer, F. (pseud.).

448. Die Juden und das deutsche Reich. Offener Brief an eine deutsche Frau. Berlin, 1879. 8vo. pp. 43. **P.**

Saint-Yves d'Alveydre.

448a. Mission des juifs. Par l'auteur de *la Mission des Souverains*. Paris, 1884 (C. Levy). 8vo. pp. 947. **P.**
[Said to be King Louis of Bavaria.]

Salaman, C. K.

449. Jews as they are. London, 1882 (Simpkin, Marshall). 8vo. pp. 314. **P.**
[VII. Persecution of Jews in Russia, pp. 259-314.]

San Donato, Prince Demidoff.

449a. The Jewish Question in Russia. Translated by J. Michell, H.M. Consul at St. Petersburg. London, 1884 (Darling). 8vo. pp. x. and 105, and Tables. **P.**
[With Preface by H. Guedalla, under whose auspices the translation was undertaken.]

Salzburger, Max.

450. L'Antisémitisme en Allemagne. Brussels, 1880. 8vo. pp. 18. (H. B. xxi. 52.) **P.**

Samuel, Mark.

450a. How to Promote and Develope Agricultural Pursuits among the Jews. Liverpool, 1883 (Marples). 8vo. pp. 11. **P.**

Sanders, Daniel [the Lexicographer].

451. Die beiden Apostel. Ein Schwank von Hans *Sachs* dem Jüngern. Zurich, 1881. 8vo. pp. 8. ("Das gelungene Gedichtchen," St. H. B. xxi. 52.) **P.**

Schein, Lazar.

451a. Blood Accusation in Roumania [Roumanian]. In *Annuar pentru israeliti* for 1882–3. Bucharest, 1882. **P.**

Scherdlin, E.

452. Le Judaisme Moderne. Extrait de l'*Encyclopédie des Sciences Religieuses*. Paris, 1882. 8vo. pp. 30. **P.**

Schiller-Szinessy, Dr. S. M.

453. Persecution of the Jews in Russia. Speech delivered at the meeting at the Guildhall, Cambridge, Feb. 15, 1882. Cambridge (Deighton, Bell & Co.), 1883. **P.**

Schleiden, Dr. M. J.

454. Die Bedeutung der Juden für die Erhaltung und Wieder belebung der Wissenschaften im Mittelalter. Leipzig, 1877 (Baumgarten). **P.**

[Abdruck aus Westermann's Monatshefte, Oct. and Nov. 1876. French Translation, Les juifs et la science au moyen age. Paris, 1877. Baer. 12mo. pp. 83. Italian Translation, Gl' Israeliti in rapporto alla scienza nel Medievo tradotto da G. Lattes. Milano, 1879.]

455. Die Romantik des Martyriums bei den Juden im Mittelalter. Leipzig, 1878 (Engelmann). 8vo. pp. 64. **P.**

Schleinitz, A. von.

456. An die Judenverfolger! Zur Entgegnung auf das Buch "Israel und die Gojinn." Berlin, 1881 (Stuhr). 8vo. pp. 51. **P.**

Schnörerer, Ritter von.

457. An Anti-Semitic pamphlet by this member of the Extreme Left of the Austrian Reichsrath was confiscated by the Vienna police, Sept. 1881. **A.**

Schönwald, Alfred.

457a. Das Drama von Tisza-Eszlar. Erinnerungsblätter an den Nyiregyhazaer Prozess. Wien, 1883 (A. Schönwald). With 50 Illustrations. **P.**

Scholl, Carl [Prediger in Nürnberg].

458. Das Judenthum und seine Weltmission [motto from Lessing "Die Juden" Vorrede]. Separatabdruck aus "Es werde Licht! Monatsblätter zur Förderung der Humanität." Jahrg. xi. (1880), Februarheft. Leipzig, 1880 (Friese). 8vo. pp. 26. **P.**

459. Das Judenthum und die Religion der Humanitäto Vortrag. Leipzig, 1879. 8vo. pp. 24. **P.**

460. Jesus von Nazareth auch ein Semite. Leipzig, 1881 (R. Friese). 8vo. pp. 23. **P.**

Schreiber, Dr. E. (Rabbiner in Bonn).

461. Grätz's Geschichtschreiberei beleuchtet von Dr. E. S. Berlin, 1881 (Issleib). 8vo. pp. iv. and 108. **P.**

462. Die Principien des Judenthums verglichen mit denen des Christenthums zur Abwehr der neueren judenfeindlichen Angriffe. Leipzig, 1877. 8vo. pp. x. and 252. **P.**

463. Die Selbstkritik der Juden. Berlin (Carl Duncker). 8vo. pp. xvi. and 167. **P.**

464. Der Talmud vom Standpunkte des modernen Judenthums. Berlin, 1881 (Issleib). 8vo. pp. 1 and 52. **P.**

Schrenzel, M.

465. Die Lösung der Judenfrage. Allen Angehörigen des jüdischen Stammes zur Beherzigung empfohlen. Lemberg, 1881 (Selbstverlag). 8vo. pp. 16. **A.**

466. Nachtrag zur Broschüre "Die Lösung der Judenfrage." Lemberg, 1881 (Selbstverlag). 8vo. pp. 14. **A.**

Schüler, G. A.

467. Die Judenfrage. Eine Frage an das deutsche Volk und die deutschen Juden. Marburg 1880 (Elwert). 8vo. pp. 85.   C.

468. Die Wurzeln der Judenfrage. Christen und Juden zunächst den Studenten Deutschlands dargelegt. Berlin, 1881 (Deut. Evang. Tractat-Gesellschaft). 8vo. pp. 60. **C.**

Von Schulte, Prof.

468b. The Religious Condition of Germany, in *Contemporary Review*, Aug. 1879.   **A.**

Schulze, P.

469. Eine Stimme aus dem Volke über die Judenfrage Cöln, 1880. 8vo. pp. 47. [H. B. xx. 33.]   ? **A.**

Schuster, Ernest.

470. The Anti-Jewish Agitation in Germany, in *Fortnightly Review*, March 1881, pp. 371-384.   **P.**

[Impartial summary, giving (1) persons engaged; (2) alleged faults of Jews; (3) how Jews are said to be detrimental to Germany; (4) practical measures proposed; (5) how the movement is met by Jews.]

Schwab, Isaac.

471. Can Jews be Patriots? An historical study. New York, 1878. 8vo. pp. 45.   **P.**
[Answer to Goldwin Smith, q.v.]

Schwabacher, Dr. Simeon Leon v. (Stadtrabbiner in Odessa).

472. Denkschrift über Entstehung und Character der in den südlichen Provinzen Russland vorgefallenen Unruhen. Stuttgart, 1882 (Levy and Müller). 8vo. pp. 43.   **P.**

Serberling, Josef.

473. Gegen Brafmann's Buch der Kahal. Erste Lieferung. Wien, 1882 (Selbstverlag). 8vo. pp. 73.
[Against No. 106.]

Siecke, Dr. Ernst.

474. Die Judenfrage und der Gymnasiallehrer. Ein Beitrag zur Richtigstellung der öffentlichen Meinung. Zweite Auflage. Berlin, 1880 (Luckhardt). 8vo. pp. 23. [Cf. No. 175.] **A.**

Seigfried, Heinrich.

475. Zwei Betrachtungen über die Antisemitenbewegung in Deutschland. Herausgegeben von H. S. Berlin. 1881 (Freund und Jeckel). 8vo. pp. x. and 36. **P.**

[Pref. by H. S. pp. i-x. Eine französische Abfertigung der Marr und Genossen. pp. 3-13, and A. Bernstein *Ein Wort zur Juden-frage* (from "Berliner Volkszeitung" Nov. 1880), pp. 15-36.]

Simonyi, Iván.

475a. Mentsuk meg a magyar földbirtskot. Orszag-gülési beszél, 1881 Okt 13-án. Pressburg, 1881 (Drovtleff). 8vo. pp. 18. (K.) **A.**
[Let us save the soil of Hungary. Speech in Parliament, 13 Oct. 1881.]

475b. Der Judaismus und die parlamentarische Komödie. Pressburg, 1882 (Drovtleff). 8vo. pp. 94. (K.) **A.**

475c. Die Wahrheit über die Judenfrage. Zu Nutz und Frommen des jüdischen Publikums. Pressburg, 1882. 8vo. pp. 125. (K.) **A.**

Simplex, Justus.

476. Der Anti-Verjüdelungsverein. Ein Komisches Epos in 10 Gesängen. Berlin, 1880 (Staude). 8vo. pp. v. and 111. **P.**

477. Werden und Vergehen des Anti-Verjudelungs-vereins. Ein harmloser Beitrag zur modernen Judenbewegung in lustigen Reimen, 2 Auflage. Berlin, 1881 (Stande). **P.**

Simplicissimus, Simplicius (Pseudonym).

478. Der Fall Kantorowicz als Sympton unserer Zustände. Eine Neujahrsbetrachtung auf Grund harmlosen Quellen-studien. Berlin, 1881 (Ruppel). 8vo. pp. 67 and Cartoon. **A.**

[Containing Anti-Semitic petition, and quotations and portraits from Frederick the Great, Kant, Schopenhauer, Schiller, Fichte, Bismark, Luther, Herder, Goethe, Wagner, Virchow, Mommsen, also the "Erklärung gegen die Petition."]

Singer, Isidor.

479. Berlin, Wien und der Antisemitismus. Wien, 1881
(Löwy). 8vo. pp. 34. P.

[Prince Bismark commenced an action against the author for the
use of his name. The Burgomaster of Vienna sent a complimentary
letter to him for the manner in which the conduct of the Viennese
was spoken of, and ordered a copy to be placed in the Municipal
Library.]

480. Presse und Judenthum. Mit einem Briefe Mr.
Lawrence Oliphants an den Verfasser. [In English.]
Wien, 1882 (Löwy). 8vo. pp. 6 and 163. P.

[List of Jewish Journals, pp. 157-163.]

480a. Sollen die Juden Christen werden? Ein offenes
Wort an Freund und Feind. Mit einem facsimilirten
Schreiben Renan's. Zweite vermehrte Ausgabe. Wien,
1884 (Frank). 8vo. pp. 138 and v. P.

Smith, Goldwin.

481. England's Abandonment of the Protectorate of
Turkey, in *Contemporary Review*, Feb. 1878. pp. 617,
618. A.

[Answered by Dr. Hermann Adler, No. 1.]

482. Can Jews be Patriots? In *Nineteenth Century*,
May, 1878, pp. 875-887. A.

[Expanding above in reply to Dr. Adler, No. 1.]

483. The Jewish Question, in *Nineteenth Century*, Oct.
1881, pp. 494-515. A.

[Answered by Dr. H. Adler, No. 3.]

484. The Jews; a Deferred Rejoinder; in *Nineteenth
Century*, Nov. 1882. A.

Sokolow, N.

485. Sinath 'olam le'am 'olam. Der uralte Hass
gegen das Urvolk, die Entstehung und Entwicklung des
Judenhasses vom Standpunkte der Geschichte und der
Psychologie. Warsaw, 1882 (Goldmann). 8vo. pp. xi.
and 212. P.

[In Hebrew.]

Somerville, Dr. A. N. (aus Glasgow).

486. Judentum und Christentum. Ein Vortrag. In revidiertem deutschem Texte herausgegeben von Franz Delitzsch. Erlangen, 1882 (Deichert). 8vo. pp. 25. **C.**

Songbook.

486a. Antisemitische Harfenklänge. Illustrirtes humoristiches Taschenliederbuch. Berlin, 1883 (M. Schulze). 8vo. with 40 Silhouettes. **A.**

Sonshein.

487. Zur Judenfrage, 1880. **P.**

Spangenberg, Max.

488. Der Standpunkt der "Freien wissenschaftlichen Vereinigung an der Universität Berlin." Zur Judenfrage und zur Wissenschaft. Zwei Reden gehalten am 4 Juli, 1881, und 30 Oct. 1882. Berlin, 1882 (Lehmann). 8vo. pp. 35. **P.**

Spitzer, S.

488a. Das Blutgespenst auf seine wahre Quelle zurückgeführt. Essek, 1883 (Pfeiffer). 8vo. pp. 20. **P.**

Stanojević, Simon.

488b. Die Wirkung der jüdischen Sittenlehre in der menschlichen Gesellschaft. II. Aufl. Zombor, 1880. 8vo. pp. 31 (K). **A.**

488c. Die Judenfrage vom slavischen Standpunkte. Szalolcza, 1881. 16mo. pp. 32 (K). **A.**

Statutes.

489. Statuten der Anti-Semitten-Liga. Bureau: Berlin, S. Prinzen Str. 48 I. Berlin. O. Hentze, Oct. 1879. 16mo. pp. 7 [containing §§ 19]. **A.**

490. Statuten-Entwurf des Central Vereins des Nichtjuden-Bundes von Ungarn. Ausgearbeitet vom Ungarischen Reichstag-Abgeordneten Victor Istoczy. Berlin [1880], O. Hentze. 16mo. pp. 12. **A.**
[Exactly in same form as Statutes of Antisemitic League, containing §§ 17.]

Stein, Dr. Leopold, Rabbiner.

491. Bileam, eine semitische Stimme. Frankfurt a/M.
1881 (Mahlau u. Waldschmidt). 12mo. pp. 16 [in
verse]. **P.**

Stein, Dr. Ludwig.

492. Berthold Auerbach und das Judenthum. Berlin,
Duessner, 1882. 8vo. pp. 40. **P.**

Steinthal, Prof.. H.

493. Ueber religiöse und nationale Vorurtheile, in *Deutsche
Revue*, 1879, pp. 189–206. [H.B. xx. 33.] **P.**

Stein, Ludwig.

494. Die Lehrsätze des neugermanischen Judenhasses
mit besonderer Rücksicht auf W. Marr's Schriften,
historisch und sachlich beleuchtet. Zweite Auflage.
Würzburg, 1879 (Stahel). 8vo. pp. iv. and 63. **P.**

Stöcker, A. (Hof- und Domprediger zu Berlin).

495. Das Moderne Judenthum in Deutschland besonders
in Berlin. Zwei Reden an die christlich-sociale Arbeiterpartei. Fünfte Auflage. Berlin, 1880 (Wiegandt u.
Grieben). 8vo. pp. 40. **A.**

496. Herr Stöcker's Rede im Lichte der Wahrheit (22
November, 1880). Berlin, 1880 (Barthel). 8vo. pp. 33.
Double columns (left Stöcker, right "Widerlegung.")
A.

497. Das moderne Judenthum in Deutschland besonders
in Berlin. Zwei Reden an die christlich-sociale
Arbeiterpartei. (Erste Auflage, ohne Vorrede.) Berlin,
1880 (Wiegandt u. Grieben). 8vo. pp. 79. **A.**

498. Dir Selbstvertheidigung des modernen Judenthums.
Rede. Staatssocialist, N. 4, 1880. 8vo. pp. 3. [H. B.
xx. 79.] **A.**

499. Social-demokratisch, Socialistisch und Christlich-
social. Braunschweig, 1880. [H. B. xx. 79.] **A.**

Stöcker A.—*continued.*

500. Wie haben Deutsche und Christen sich gegen die judischen Mitbürger zu verhalten? Brief des Herrn Hofprediger Stöcker. Berlin (F. Starcke). Broadsheet, 4to. pp. 2. **A.**

Stöpel, Franz.

501. Apologie der Juden von einem Germanen, in "Merkur," first Heft, Jan. 1880, pp. 1–37. [H. B. xx. 33.] **P.**
[Cf. Anon.]

Sulpicius (Pseudonym).

502. Der Judenhass und die Mittel zu seiner Beseitigung. Ein ernstes Mahnwort an unsere Zeit. Wesentlich erweiterter Separatabdruck aus der Allgemeinen Montagspresse. Zweite Auflage. Stuttgart, 1882 (Fröhner). 12mo. pp. 16. **P.**

Sulzbach, Dr. A.

503. Rischuss oder Judenidiosynkrasie. Eine Zeitstudie. Loebau, 1879 (Skrzeczek). 8vo. pp. iv. and 39. **P.**

Sulzberger, M.

503a. Persecution of Jews in Germany. In *Penn Monthly*, vol. xii. p. 100. 1881. **P.**

Swinburne, Algernon Charles.

504. Sonnet in *Daily Telegraph*, Feb. 1st, 1882, "On the Persecution of the Jews in Russia" (reproduced in *Tristan of Lyonnesse and other Poems*, 1882). **P.**

Taussig, F. W.

504a. Movement against Jews in Germany, 1880. *Nation*, vol. xxx. p. 468. New York. **P.**

Timann, Richard.

505. Die Judenfrage und die evangelische Kirche. Ein Wort des Bekenntnisses und der Mahnung. Halle a. d. S., 1881. [H. B. xxi. 52.] **P.**

Trapp, und Maas.

505a. Die Isaakiade. Oder der Ewige Jude des XIXten Jahrhunderts. **A.**

[The authors (? publisher) were prosecuted for this *brochure*, See *Jew. Chr.* 4 Dec. 1884.]

Treitschke, Heinrich von.

506. Ein Wort über unser Judenthum. (Separatabdruck aus dem 44 und 45 Bande der Preussischen Jahrbücher.) Berlin, 1880 (Reimer). 8vo. pp. i. and 27. **A.**

507. Erwiderung an Herrn Th. Mommsen, in *Preussische Jahrbücher*, Dec. 1880. **A.**

508. Die jüdische Einwanderung in Deutschland, in *Preussische Jahrbücher*, Jan. 1881.

[In answer to Neumann, No. 326, answered by the same in *Nachschrift.*]

V., C. P.

509. La question des Israélites devant de congrés et devant la Roumanie, par C. P. V. Roumanie et électeur du premier college de Romanatz. Bucarest, 1878. 16mo. pp. 13. [H. B. xviii. 57.] **P.**

Valbert, G. (=Victor Cherbuliez).

510. La question des Juifs en Allemagne, in *Revue des Deux-Mondes*, 1st March, 1880. **P.**

[Reproduced in *Hommes et Choses de mon Temps*, Paris, 1883.]

510a. L'affaire de Tisza-Ezlar, in *Revue des Deux-Mondes*, 1st April, 1883, pp. 681–92. **P.**

Vambery, H.

511. Die Juden in Orient, in *Deutsche Revue*, 1879, pp. 61–67. **P.**

Vindex, Dr. Carl.

512. Zeit- und Cultur-Bilder II. Antisemitische Wühlereien und Raufereien in Pleiss-Athen. Ein Beitrag zur Culturgeschichte unserer Zeit. Leipzig, 1881. (Expedition d. Z. C. B.) 8vo. pp. 47. **P.**

Wagner, Richard.

513. In *Bayreuther Blätter*, 28th May, 1881. **A.**

[Cf. his *Das Judenthum in der Musik*, 1869; cf. Cassel, No. 130, V., C. F. Glassenapp and H. von Stein, *Wagner-Lexikon*, 1883, sub vocc. *Gebildeheit, Juden, Judenemancipation, Das Judenthum in der Musik, Moderne Presse*.]

Wahrmund, Dr. Adolf.

514. Babyloniertum Judenthum und Christenthum. Leipzig, 1882 (Brockhaus). 8vo. pp. xi. and 294. **A.**

Waldegg, Egon.

515. Judenhetze oder Nothwehr? Dresden, 1880 (Verlag d. Reform Vereins und O. Hentze). 8vo. pp. 31. **A.**

516. Die Judenfrage. Ein Manifest an die deutsche Nation gegenüber dem deutschen Handel und Gewerbe. 5te. theilweise veränderte Auflage. Dresden, 1880 (Grumbkow). **A.**

Wasinski, A.

517. Die Situation. Erste Extrafahrt der Dampfwatze. Berlin, 1880 (O. Lorenz). 8vo. pp. 19. **A.**

[cf. Poster. — Containing 1. Die Entstehung des Konservativ-Antisemitischen Bündnisses; 4 Die Berechtigung der antisemitischen Idee.]

Wedell, R. A. C. v.

518. Vorurtheil oder ferechtigter Hass? Eine vortheilslose Besprechung der Judenfrage. Berlin, 1880 (O. Hentze). 8vo. pp. 44. **A.**

Weiss, Siegfried.

519. Trente Ans de Persecutions par les Juifs pour ma conversion au Christianisme. Première Partie. Paris, 1877 (chez tous les libraires). 8vo. pp. 64. **A.**

Wertheimer, Joseph Ritter von.

520. Zur Emancipation unserer Glaubensgenossen. Wien, 1882 (Waitzner). 8vo. pp. 29. **P.**

Γ [This pamphlet, written on the author's 80th birthday, was seized by the Berlin police.]

Wertheimer, J. R. von—*continued.*

520a. Jüdische Lehre und jüdisches Leben mit besonderer Beziehung auf die Juden von Oesterreich und auf die Pflichten gegen Vaterland und Mitmenschen. Wien, 1883 (Hölder). 8vo. pp. 34. **P.**

[Containing criminal statistics of Austrian Jews 1875-82, p. 25 seq. Translated into Hebrew by H. Zupnik (Drohobycz).]

Wieninger, Adolf.

521. Selbsthilfe gegen die fortschreitende Verjudung und Verarmung unseres Volkes. Vienna, 1881. 8vo. [H. B. xxi. 53.] **A.**

Willheimer, Jonas.

522. Der Judenhass. Wien, 1881. **P.**

Witt, A.

523. Die Juden in ihrer socialen und bürgerlichen Stellung. Augsburg, 1879 (Selbstverlag). 12mo. pp. 22. **P.**

Wolf, Lucien.

524. A Jewish View of the Anti-Jewish Agitation (on *Judenhetze* in Germany), in *Nineteenth Century*, Feb. 1881, pp. 338-357. **P.**

525. Notes on Modern Jews, in *Leisure Hour*, June, 1882, pp. 372-76 ; July, 1882, pp. 440-44. **P.**

525a. What is Judaism? A question of To-day, in *Fortnightly Review*, Aug. 1884, pp. 237-256. **P.**

Wolff, A. A.

526. Talmudfjender. Et genmaele mod de seneste angreb paa Joderne og Jodedomen. Copenhagen, 1878. 8vo. pp. iv. and 504. [H. B. xviii. 106.] **P.**

Wolff (Lehrer in Kuppenheim).

527. Ein Wort der Verwahrung und zur Abwehr. Karlsruhe, 1874. 8vo. pp. 40. [H. B. xx. 34.] **P.**

Wolff, Lion.

527a. Wucher und Intoleranz. Eine Antwort auf die Schrift von Marr. ? 1879.   **P.**

Wilmanns, C.

528. Die "goldene" Internationale und die Nothwendigkeit einer socialen Reformpartei. Berlin, 1876 (Niendorf). 8vo. pp. 107.   **A.**

Wright, Rev. C. H. H.

528a. The Jews and the Malicious Charge of Human Sacrifice. In *Nineteenth Century*, Nov. 1883, pp. 753-78.   **P.**

[Giving account of Tisza-Eszlar trial, and analysing controversy between Delitzsch and Rohling; cf. No. 154a and 437.]

Wyking, A.

529. Die Juden Berlins nach historischen Quellen bearbeitet. Berlin, 1882 (Lorentz). 8vo. pp. 63.   **A.**

Zander, C.

530. Handbuch enthaltend die sämmtlichen Bestimmungen über die Verhältnisse der Juden im Preussischen Staate. Leipzig, 1881 (Scholtze). 8vo. pp. xxii. and 124.

APPENDIX.

[Mostly 1883-4.]

Altlass, Osias.

531. *Hanardef mi'arez Russia.* Der Verfolgte von Russland : Ein Trauerspiel in 3 Aufzügen. Przemysl (Galicia), 1884. (Drama in Hebrew.)   **P.**

Anon.
532. Apion, Roman aus dem ersten christlichen Jahrhundert. 1883. **P.**

533. Eingabe der 3 Vertheidiger Eötvös Funták Horanszky in der Tisza-Eszlarer Augelegenheit. Budapest, 1883 (Markus). 8vo. pp. 68 (K). **P.**

534. Istóczy und Onody. Budapest, 1882 (Neuer). 8vo. pp. 11 (K.) **P.**

535. A magyar-zsidó kérdés jogi társadalmi s nemzetisegi zempontból. Budapest, 1882. 8vo. pp. 32 (K). **P.**
[The Hungarian Jewish Question from a legal, social, and historic point of view.]

536. Der Mord von Tisza Eszlár besprochen von einem evangelischen Priester. Budapest, 1882. 8vo. pp. 30 (K). **P.**

537. Die Teufelskralle. Eine düstere Erzählung von Früher für Jetzt. Zur Geschichte des "Blutopfers." Leipzig, 1884 (Kössling). 8vo. pp. 36. **P.**
[Written by a Roman Catholic, and giving instances of blood-sacrifices among Christians in 1814.]

538. A Zsidókérdés Magyarorszagon. Röpirat melyben bebizonyittalik, rogy a müvelt zsidók áttérése valamelyik protestans vallazra, erkölcsileg igazolt eo nagy, polilikai érdekek által sürgetett eljárás. Budapest, 1882 (L. Kokai). 8vo. pp. 31 (K). **C.**
[The Jewish Question in Hungary. Brochure in which it is proved that the conversion of the Jews to a Protestant belief is morally justified and earnestly demanded by great political interests.]

Astruc, Aristide (Grand Rabbin).
539. Conference sur les causes et les origines historiques de l'anti-semitisme. **P.**
In *Annuaire de la Société des etudes juives*, 3me Année, 1884, pp. 113-162.

Baum, Jacob.
540. Der Talmud im ungarischen Abgeordnetenhause Budapest, 1882. 8vo. pp. 14 (K). **P.**

Baum, Moritz.

541. Ein wichtiges Kapitel oder Abhandlung über die Bedeutung und Würde nach den Gesetzen der Thora der Völker unserer Zeit sowie der Vorzeit, im Talmud gewöhnlich "Akum" genannt. Selbstverlag. Frankfurt a/M, 1884. 8vo. pp. 64. **P.**

["Akum"=those who do not keep the 7 Noachic commands.]

Boole, Mrs. Mary.

542. Jews and Gentiles. 8vo. pp. 7. **P.**

[Reprinted from *Jew. Chron.* of 14th Nov. and 5 Dec. 1884.]

Cappilleri, W.

543. Die Antisemiten. Episches Zeitgedicht. Vienna, 1884. (D. Löwy). **P.**

[81 quatrains]

Cassel, Dr. Paulus.

544. Ahasuerus. Die Sage vom ewigen Juden. Eine wissenschaftliche Abhandlung. Mit einem kritischen Protest gegen Ed. v. Hartmann und Adolf Stöcker. Berlin, 1885 (Gerstmann). **P.**

T. D. Daniow.

545. The Prussian Anti-Semitic League, in *Catholic World*, 33, 131. 1881. **P.**

Ecker, Jakob.

546. Der "Judenspiegel" im Lichte der Wahrheit. Eine wissenschaftliche Untersuchung. Paderborn (1884), (Bonifacius-Druckreri). 4to. pp. xvii. and 74. **A.**

Eismann, M. J. A.

547. *B'pera' pera'oth b'Yisra'el.* (Observations on the Jews of Russia and the uselessness of the means proposed to relieve their misery.) Warsaw, 1883 (Hirs). 8vo. pp. 135 and 1. **P.**

[In Hebrew. Deprecates America, and advises Palestine as asylum.]

Friedländer, M. H.

548. Zur Geschichte der Blutbeschuldigungen gegen die Juden. 2 Aufl. Brünn, 1883 (Epstein). 8vo. pp. 36. **P.**

Frank, Arnold (Licentiate of the Irish Presbyterian Church).

549. The Jewish Problem and its Solution. Belfast (Mullan), 1883. 16mo. pp. 54. **C.**

Geist, Karl.

550. Die Strassentumulte in Pressburg. Budapest, 1882. 8vo. pp. 24 (K). **P.**

Gildemeister, Prof.

551. Der Schulchan Aruch und was daran hängt. Ein gerichtlich-gefordertes Gutachten. Bonn, 1884. [Answered by Hoffmann, No. 557, Joel No. 558.] **A.**

Groebler, F.

552. Das Blutopfer der talmudischen Juden, eine Untersuchung der Frage ob dieselben Christenblut zu geheimen Zwecken gebrauchen und ob der Talmud den Christenmord gestattet oder sogar zur Pflicht macht. Munich 1883 (Kramer). 8vo. pp. 15. **P.**

Guidetti, Corrado.

553. Pro Judæis, riflessioni et documenti. Turin, 1884 (Roux). 8vo. pp. 386. **P.**
[Very complete on blood-accusation.]

Hall, G. Stanley.

554. Persecution of Jews in Germany, in *Nation*, 1879, vol. 30, p. 74. **P.**

Hartmann, E. von.

555. Das Judenthum in Gegenwart und Zukunft. Sozial-Politische Abhandlungen. 8vo. Berlin, 1884. **A.**

Hirsch, Rabbiner S. R.

556. Ueber die Beziehung des Talmuds zum Judenthum und zu der sozialen Stellung seiner Bekenner. Frankfurt a/M. 1884 (Kaufmann). 8vo. pp. 38. **P.**

Hoffmann, Dr. D.

557. Der Schulchan Aruch und die Rabbinen über das Verhältniss der Juden zu andersgläubigen. Zur Berichtigung des von Prof. Gildemeister in "Isaakiade" Prozess abgegebenen Gutachtens. Berlin, 1885 ("Jüd. Presse"). 8vo. pp. 160. **P.**

Joel, Dr. M.

558. Gegen Gildemeister. Herrn Prof. Gildemeister's Gutachten über den jüdischen Ritualcodex (Schulchan Aruch) und das Verhältniss der Juden zu demselben Buche. Breslau (Schottländer), 1884. 16mo. pp. 34. **P.**

Justus, Dr. (pseudonym = Breimann).

559. Talmudische Weisheit, 400 höchst interessante märchenhafte Aussprüche der Rabbinen, direct aus der Quelle geschöpft und dem christlichen Volke vorgetragen. Paderborn, 1884 (Bonifacius Druckerei). **A.**

Laube, Heinrich.

560. Ruben. Roman. Leipzig, 1885. **P.**

Lazarus, Prof. Dr. M.

561. Einiges aus den Motiven welche in der Coblenzer Conferenz von 11 und 12 August, 1883, zu dem Beschluss geführt haben ein grundlegendes Werk über jüdische Ethik ins Leben zu rufen. (Als Manuscript gedruckt). 1884. 8vo. pp. 8. **P.**

Levi, David.

562. Il semitismo nella civiltà dei popoli. Turin, 1884. 8vo. pp. 92. **P.**

Lewin, Dr. Adolf (Rabbiner in Coblenz).

563. Der Judenspiegel des Dr. Justus in's Licht der Wahrheit gerückt. Magdeburg, 1884 ('Isr. Wochenschrift.') 8vo. pp. 89. **P.**
[An answer to Justus, No. 251a, taking each of the 100 laws quoted in that work.]

Lippe, Dr. K.

564. Der Talmudjude vor dem katholisch-protestantisch-orthodoxen Dreirichter-Kollegium : Rohling, Stöcker, Pobedonoscew. Pressburg, 1884. 8vo. pp. 41. **P.**

Lipschutz, J. Levi.

565. *Lepter dibré shalom v'emeth.* (On the mission of Rabbis in Russia and the utility of a capable body of Rabbis.) Warsaw, 1884 (Hins). 8vo. pp. 62. **P.**
[In Hebrew.]

Löwy, D.

566. Der Talmudjude von Rohling. Wien, 1883. (D.
Löwy). **P.**

Müller, Dr. Alois.

566a. Brauchen die Juden Christenblut? Eine Oster-
gabe an denkende Christen. Wien, 1885 (Frank). **P.**

Neumann, Dr. S.

567. Die neueste Lüge über die israelitische Allianz.
Berlin, 1883. **P.**
[A forged speech attributed to M. Crémieux.]

568. Zur Statistik der Juden in Prussen von 1816 bis
1880. Zweiter Beitrag aus den amtlichen Veröffentli-
chungen. Berlin, 1884 (Gerschel). 8vo. pp. 50. **P.**
[Dedicated to Zunz on his ninetieth birthday 10th Aug. 1884. A
second appendix to No. 326.]

Ronge, Joannes.

568a. Offenes Sendschreiben an die geistlichen Mitglie-
der des Antisemiten-Congresses. Darmstadt, 16 Jan.
1881. 4to. pp. 4. **P.**

Schmeitzner.

569. Internationale Monatsschrift. Zeitschrift für die
allgem. Vereinigung zur Bekämpfung des Judenthums,
Alliance antijuive universelle. Chemnitz, 1882. In progress. **A.**

Sello, Dr. [Rechtsanwalt].

570. Der Neustettiner Synagogenbrand—Prozess. Mit
einem Situations-plan der Synagoge und Umgebung. In
Das Tribunal No. I. Jan. 1885. pp. 5–58. **P.**

Stöcker, A.

571. Die Berliner Juden und das öffentliche Leben
Reden gehalten in der Versammlung Deutscher Bürger . . . am 2 Juli, 1883. 4to. pp. 8. **A.**

STEPHEN AUSTIN AND SONS, PRINTERS, HERTFORD.

www.ingramcontent.com/pod-product-compliance
Ingram Content Group UK Ltd.
Pitfield, Milton Keynes, MK11 3LW, UK
UKHW042150280225
455719UK00001B/252